Reminiscences of Louise Romberg Fuchs 1927

Translated from the German

by

Helen and Gertrude Franke

1936

Revised
by
Kenneth W. Fuchs
2010

Supplementary notations taken from

The Golden Free Land

by Crystal Sasse Ragsdale

Landmark Press
Austin, Texas 1976

Reminiscences of Louise Romberg Fuchs 1927
Translated from the German by Helen and Gertrude
Franke 1936. Revised by Kenneth W. Fuchs 2010
Supplementary notations taken from *The Golden Free
Land* by Crystal Sasse Ragsdale — Landmark Press
Austin, Texas 1976
ISBN: 978-3-949197-10-9

© 2020 Texianer Verlag
www.texianer.com

The publishers are most grateful for the material provided by Kenneth Fuchs, the work painstakingly carried out by his family and the support he has given to this project of preserving this valuable historic document. Cover Photo: Wilhelma and Louise Fuchs by courtesy of Kenneth Fuchs.

Contents

Introduction	5
My Parents	7
My Childhood in Germany	9
Departure from Germany in the Year 1847	13
The Voyage	15
In Texas	17
Friends And School	21
Three Weddings and Departure from the San Bernard	31
Old Remembrances	33
On the Navidad	39
Travels by Horse and Wagon	45
Engagements and Weddings	53
To My Home in the Mountains	59
Our Home Near the Pedernales	85
Appendices	123
Mothers of the Nineteenth Century	123
Reminiscences of Theodora Hoppe Fuchs	131
At Grandfather's by Helene Romberg Mackensen	137
Biographical Sketch	141
Johannes Christlieb Nathanael Romberg German Poet Of Texas	149
The Story Of The Romberg Family	159

Introduction

We, who live in the Machine Age, can scarcely imagine how our grandparents and parents, who came from a populous country, the home of their parents, and moved with them to the thinly settled state of Texas, passed their youth—under circumstances and surroundings so entirely different from those under which we grandchildren and children live.

Therefore, we gladly listen when Grandmother or Grandfather tells of that time: the pioneer days with their sorrows and joys!

And so the children and grandchildren of Louise Fuchs have asked her to write down her Reminiscences, so that those days will not vanish for us in the stream of time.

Frieda H. Fuchs

My Parents

My father, Johannes Christlieb Nathanael Romberg, was the only son and only child of a minister Bernhard Friedrich Christlieb Romberg, and as was then the custom, he was also intended for the ministry; but weak eyes, the result of measles, made it hard for him to study. He felt an inclination to learn a trade, but the social standards of that time forbade that a minister's son should do manual labor; so it was decided by his elders that he should become a merchant, for which calling he had neither talent nor inclination. While yet quite young he entered the business house of the merchant Johannes Dietrich Bauch for training.

Bauch's second oldest daughter Friederike later became our mother. He was very shy and timid and my mother, still a child, felt sympathy for his loneliness. And I know not how it happened they soon became good friends. In his leisure hours she read to him, and frequently they discussed what they had read. He was a thinker and ponderer. She was planning to become a teacher, and she developed into a remarkably clever woman who was a match for any educated person in a discussion. I well remember this, for in our American "Settlement" lived many well-educated neighbors: a minister, an officer, a physician, an attorney, etc.

At the age of fourteen years Friederike became engaged to Johannes Romberg. Then she left her father's house to teach, and it was in her twenty-fourth year (1833) that they married. They lived in Boizenburg on the Elbe, where my father started his own business (1833). Here four daughters and two sons came into the world—I in the year 1840.

My father never took pleasure in his business, but when he had a chance to do some cabinet- or brick-work in or on the house, he did it gladly. He was a tradesman unwillingly; he liked writing poetry much better. He also enjoyed working in the garden. Later on in America Mother had to attend to all the business.

My Childhood in Germany

Since I have always had so much affection for anything that had to do with the land, I must also tell you of the nice garden which we had on the edge of the town; it gave me so much pleasure, and is still such a bright spot in my memory! In it grew apples, pears, plums, and different berries.

Entirely through the garden ran a broad path, on each side of which beautiful roses grew. Early in the spring there were tulips, hyacinths, and many other flowers, but the lily-of-the-valley was the earliest. I still remember my joy when I found the first blossom half covered with snow, while in the blue spring sky several white clouds floated, and a crow called his "Caw, Caw!" down from above. And whenever I hear this "Caw, Caw!" again, I think of that spring morning.

On each side of the entrance stood a plum tree—the large blue plum—and as we stepped into the garden one morning, the ground was covered with the dark, ripe plums; how we shouted for joy! Such a sight I have never seen over here.

Our father had a grocery store, but as he had an assistant to help him he had some time for other things. When there was something in the house that needed to be altered or that had to be made, he always did it. Once he built a heater for our dining room, using tiles. (Here no one knows that building stone). For us children he made various toys which gave him, as well as us, pleasure.

He also manufactured vinegar which was very good —made of honey. For that he had a special room. There everything had to be made of wood, because the vinegar vapor corrodes all iron. Large barrels of honey were used there.

We always had a little honey on our dining table. This honey was raised in the Lüneburger woodland.

Almost in front of our house was an avenue of large trees, and behind them stood the church. Our house was a corner house, to the right of which stood the business section. To the left up the street lived the high constable (Amtshauptmann) of the district; there I was often invited as a playmate for the only child, Lillie, who was my age. There I had fine times. She had so very many beautiful toys!

When they went for a drive I was often taken along; one evening a servant came for me, so that I could go with them to visit little Lillie's grandmother. That must have been the wish of my playmate; otherwise, I probably would not have been taken along. For gradually I began to find out, small as I still was, that according to the ideas of that time I was probably not a playmate of proper rank. Nevertheless, later on we corresponded for a while. But first, here in Texas, I had to learn to read and write, and that did not go so quickly, for generally Mother taught us only during the winter. In the summer there was work for us in the fields. But wait—we are not yet in Texas!

It was not till the year 1847 that we moved away. The circumstances in that populous country were such that our parents began to be concerned, as the number of their children grew, as to how they would find opportunities for all of them.—Also, the thought of living in a republic was very tempting. At that time the circumstances here were quite different; whoever was willing to work had a chance to prosper even with a large family of children. Children even were assets in the parents' struggle to advance. The demands of existence were so simple, so few; yet everyone was contented, healthy, and happy.

But once more my thoughts fly back to Germany to an uncle of my mother's, Rev. Bauch [Friedrich Wilhelm Heinrich Bauch, 1786-1866] of Zahrensdorf ["Sternsdorf" in the original German text], a German mile from Boizenburg. He was a country minister, and lived on a small stream called the Schaale. A fine garden lay between the house and the stream, with a broad path to the stream and on each side of the path rows of flowers and fruit trees. That was just what I liked! In particular I remember the beautiful blooming lilacs and the fruit we were often given to eat. And always we were taken for a boat ride down the stream, on which occasion we would go under a bridge, a very interesting adventure for me. Then we also went fishing, but the results of that I have forgotten, except that there were always fish to eat.

With what joy we always looked forward to such a visit! We rode on a fine, paved highway, and I remember we always had to stop at one place to pay toll. The money taken in was used to keep the highway repaired. The railroad also crossed the highway, and an iron chain barred the way when the train passed. That was the first train I saw.

The son of this uncle, Adolph Bauch, later traveled with us to Texas.

Departure from Germany in the Year 1847

Now I must mention how very hard it was for all of us to leave our dearly loved Grandmother Romberg, Conradine Sophie Friederike Hast. She had one relative in Germany, and she intended to live with her. She naturally clung to her only son and his family, but she felt too weak to go along and experience the hard beginning in the new land, and she feared that she would be a burden; our parents also did not like to risk taking her into such uncertain circumstances. Consequently, the bitter parting took place in Hagenow, where her only relative lived. Then came the farewells to Mother's relatives. A distant cousin went with us to the train by which we intended going to Schwerin to the relatives. (Father stayed behind on business.) At the railroad station Mother said to us children, "Sit here quietly until I come again!"

She left us only to buy the tickets, but it took too long for us, and we went to meet Mother. Then the signal was given to take our seats on the train! As we rolled off we noticed that the youngest, Ida, — the most obedient — had stayed in her place. What a "frightened and general crying" and lamentation then began. There was nothing we could do, for it was not till the next morning that our mother, leaving us with her relatives in Schwerin, would be able to get the little sister. Our cousin, who had accompanied us to the train, found her and took her home with him — a lucky ending to the story. And Mother found her at his house, comforted, and eating bread and butter.

The Voyage

I still remember the feeling that came over me after all the farewells had been said. We were finally on the way, and our little sailing vessel began to move away from Hamburg, sailing over the apparently boundless water. Once we had a strong storm, and I can still see the waves dashing about, on every wave a large fish, as if the ocean swarmed with them.

There were many things that we had to do without on the voyage. The ship bread, large brown "crackers," was almost unbearably hard. My mother made the discovery that by pounding up the crackers and adding dried fruit and sugar which she had brought along, she could prepare a right passable soup; and soon many of our fellow-voyagers were doing the same, and then there was a general pounding. Drinking water was very sparingly apportioned, and we sometimes suffered from rather dry throats.

Finally we landed in New Orleans; from there we went to Galveston in a steamboat. The voyage had taken eleven weeks, much longer than our parents had expected. On the last night we had a storm [November 17, 1847]. Our mother stayed in the cabin, while we children crawled into any corner in which we could find room together, where we tried to sleep, surrounded by lumber which rolled about us. Then an old Negro came and showed us a better place; the spot we had chosen was too dangerous, for something might have fallen on our heads.

In the morning, after a wakeful night, our aunt, Louise Bauch, who was making the voyage with us came and announced to us that the night had brought us another sister [Friederike or Rike]. Then there was great surprise and joy, and all our fatigue was forgotten.

In Texas

At daybreak we landed in Galveston, and our big, strong muscular cousin Adolf Bauch carried our mother to the shore. From there she and the little sister were taken to the hotel. How we got to Houston I do not remember any more, but I do remember that we spent four weeks there in a hotel. The room we lived in was divided by curtains.

We continued our journey inland by ox-wagon. In Houston it rained almost continually, until a north wind finally cleared the sky. Our father bought land on the River San Bernard [in Austin County], and for our first shelter got a room for us with an old Texan named [Heinrich] Amthor. There we stayed, while Father with the help of our strong cousin built a log-house. It consisted of two rooms, with a hall between. The shingles for the roof also had to be made, and I do not know how long it was before we could finally move in. In one of the rooms, likewise, a fireplace had to be built. At that time fireplaces were made of wood and clay. In it we burned many a log, while the north wind howled and blustered differently than in these days. We slept soundly, but I remember that we often heard a branch of a large post-oak tree scraping on the roof. How did we get into the garret to our bed? Father made a settee with a high back (he brought all kinds of tools along when he came over here), and from this settee we managed to climb up into the garret, and down again.

I must tell you what a splendid playground the sandy Bernard was for us children. It was so nice in the sand! There mountains were heaped up and tunnels dug through with our bare hands. Canals were dug, and the water that followed our tunnels flowed as we wished. The mounds were decorated with flowers that stayed fresh in the moist sand. If only the cattle would not come and destroy everything. That was the nicest playground for children that one could think of. In the clean, white sand the clothing stayed unsoiled, and our pleasure was endless—until we came the next day to get water for our dear mother's cooking and found everything trampled down, as was often the case. But we always built it up again, like the Japanese, who, undiscouraged, after the most awful volcanic eruption again start rebuilding.

We had to carry all the water for our household use. Later we had a barrel on a sled, which old Hans the horse had to pull. We children, several at once, found room on his broad back, for in those days there were no buggies and cars. Scarcely one old farm wagon with wooden axles was to be found. Such large horses like our Hans I never see now. Three or four of us children often found a place on his back. But frequently it became apparent that he wished to enjoy a roll in the sand. Then, when he made a motion to do so, we scrambled from all sides off his back to the ground. Our Hans was what was then called an "American horse," very large, good for plowing and driving. At that time there were also small Mexican horses for riding, but they were not quite trustworthy.

Our field was fenced in by a zigzag fence of post-oak rails. Many large dead trees still stood in our field, and in April fine blackberries ripened around the trunks or stumps. We celebrated my oldest brother's birthday, April 14, with the first berries; they were eaten with sugar and cream in later years.

It was wonderful how many plants grew voluntarily in the sandy field beside the corn: butter beans that climbed up the corn stalks, okra, squash, and pumpkins. We never had to plant any, for they always came up by themselves. In the fence corners we found tomatoes, small and round, growing in clusters.

In Texas

At that time game was very plentiful. From the house we could see the deer grazing on the other side of the Bernard and could see the turkeys in the field, with their flocks of young ones, gleaning the corn. But it was long before my brother Johannes (the oldest) learned to shoot them, and still longer before he succeeded in killing a deer, hard as he tried. How often in the spring one could often be seen from the house.

In those first years no one ever thought of hauling fire wood. We children had to gather it. Sometimes we also went along the fence and pulled off the bark from the post-oak rails. Mother like to burn this bark. We were often stung by scorpions while gathering it.

During the winter the first years we lived on beef and sweet potatoes, and very often we were without milk. But I must not forget to mention our cornbread and molasses. This is how we arranged it: The oldest sister went around with the molasses can and gave everyone a portion on the plate with cornbread, and we had to be satisfied with that. The clear river water drunk with this food tasted good to us children.

Oh, when one thinks of all that is placed on the table today! How entirely everything has changed in one lifetime! I scarcely feel at home in these changed circumstances.

On winter evenings when we all sat in a half circle before the fireplace, Father told us stories. Oh, how we enjoyed listening. Sometimes he teased us. When a very interesting situation came, he would puff thick clouds of smoke for awhile out of his long pipe, which he had brought along from Germany, and we had to wait impatiently until he let his pipe rest and took up the thread of the story again. Often he had thought out the story himself. I think that I must have inherited that gift, for later on while at work in the field I told my brothers and sisters many stories, and it was interesting to them. They listened attentively and begged for "More!" But how singular! Later when I wanted to relate something to my children, I could not do it. Work and sorrow must have killed the talent. I did not understand why I could no longer succeed in telling a story.

Friends And School

I must also tell you of our good neighbors, Amthors. We liked to visit there, and we were glad when they came to see us.—Here I must mention that now in the year 1927, a son of these Amthors', Wilhelm Amthor, is a good friend of my oldest grandson, Moritz Goebel, in Waco.—How everything has changed from 1848 to 1927! Amthors had a nice large house, approached by an avenue of huge chinaberry trees. In their shade hung swings, and there we spent many happy hours playing together. One son, Heinrich, was the age of my oldest brother, Johannes; Marie was my age. We spent so many happy hours there, and yet we drifted entirely apart when we moved away later. Therefore, I was glad that the descendants, Wilhelm Amthor and Moritz Goebel, became friends.

A family named Himli [Alex and Clothilda Himly] lived near us on the Bernard; my youngest brothers and sisters often played with the children, as they were all more or less of the same age.

It was a great event when the first piano was brought into our community. It belonged to the youngest aunt on our mother's side, Caroline Bauch, who with her mother Dorothea Schleef Bauch and a sister had immigrated from Germany. (The sister, Elise, died on the ship of cholera and was buried at sea.) During the voyage Caroline Bauch became acquainted with the engineer Getulius Kellersberger and also became engaged to him. They married at our house, and then traveled on to Mexico and California. They did not want to take the piano along, because Kellersberger as a surveyor could not have a stationary residence. He made surveys for the city of San Francisco, also in New York, Mexico, and later in Texas.

For the piano they soon found buyers. Our neighbors, Amthor and Rev. Adolf Fuchs, both wanted it very much, so they decided who was to get it by casting lots. Our neighbor Amthor won it, so it stayed near us, and frequently a musical afternoon and evening was arranged there, for Amthor was a great music lover, and he often invited Rev. Fuchs over to sing his beautiful songs. On such occasions we neighbors were always present. A male choir also often sang there or at our house., and that sounded wonderful coming through the large oak trees on those moonlight nights. Ludwig / Louis Franke, a cousin of Rev. Fuchs', often let the children sing. This Franke later became my brother-in-law.

But let me tell you some more about Rev. Fuchs and his family, because the Fuchs and Romberg families are still to this day closely associated. At that time they lived five miles from us at Cat Springs. Ottilie was the age of my oldest sister Bernhardine, while Ino [Adolfine] was my age. When they came to visit us, we played with the wonderful toy dishes and with the many beautiful dolls that I had received from my Grandmother Romberg in Germany. The dishes were so large that we could really cook with them. However, we had barely prepared a nice meal when, much too soon for us, it was time for them to leave, and everything had to be quickly packed away. Nearer neighbors with daughters my age we did not have, so it was always hard for me to part from Ino Fuchs and Marie Amthor after we had played together. But we had other

friends among our neighbors, who often on summer evening assembled under a large poplar tree in front of our house, where they rested on a large settee that Father had made. Then songs were sung, and often the men held disputes. How I enjoyed listening to both! The old tunes still ring in my head: "Im Krug zum grünenn Kranze" and "It cannot always remain so, here under the

Friends And School

changing moon; it blossoms awhile and then withers, whatever inhabits this world with us." Yes, yes, how the times have changed! Wonderful is the progress and change occurring on one lifetime. For in truth, I am old now and can scarcely relate anything coherently.

When my sister Bernhardine and Ottilie Fuchs (later Ottilie Goeth) were together, they always sat and read. That is what my sister was usually doing, for we had brought many books along and she was very fond of reading. On summer afternoons she had barely finished eating before she was deep in her reading again. Then I could stand beside her and say, "Bernhardine, let's wash the dishes!" as often as I liked. She did not hear or move: I could repeat it and shake her, but nothing disturbed her. I sometimes gave it up and attended to the dishwashing alone. At such times she lived only for her book! I was, to be sure, much stronger than she was, much healthier, and have had some work to do all my life, in the house, in the field, and in the garden. This always interested me, and I always attended to it with ardor as long as I was at home. I always had flowers in the house, too. We could not grow them in the yard because of the chickens.

My dear grandmother in Germany always sent me all kinds of flower seeds: wonderful stocks, carnations, mignonette, hyacinth bulbs, all of which were my standing favorites.

On Sunday afternoons, when the dishes were washed, I frequently went out with my younger sisters, Ida, Lina [alternately spelled "Line," short for Caroline], and Rike, (the latter our ship-baby), to a nice flowery place. There I sat down, my sisters brought me flowers, and I wove each one a wreath to adorn her head, so that in the evening all came home crowned with flowers. But often I had to use my spare time to make new clothing for their dolls. That must have been the prelude to my later life!

You must not judge from this, dear children, that I was always so gentle and industrious. No, I bet my brothers that I could beat them climbing trees, and I won! Scarcely a tree was too high for me. Oh, that seemed heavenly to me, to climb high in the trees, which were usually festooned with wild grapes. The grape vines were so strong that we could climb on them from tree to tree.

But often after hard work in the field chopping cotton (where we were bothered with crabgrass), we lay still enjoying the noon-rest and reading. Poems gave me great pleasure, and I liked to memorize them and later recite them at my work in the field, so that I would not forget them. For me it was a pleasure to rejoice in their beauty while I was working.

In our long bookshelf we had such a nice selection of books that we could read and study. My mother was an excellent reader. Many times the winter evenings seemed too short, yea, much too short. My mother knitted while she read aloud, which did not seem to disturb her in the least. On the contrary; for her reading and knitting stockings seemed to belong together. And yet we children wore shoes and stockings only when we went visiting, and then they were a torment!

I can still so distinctly hear our mother reading to us, and see the knitting needles busily twinkling also. But once in a while her hands would fell in her lap, and her voice after an indistinct murmur would become silent, her head would nod, and she would sleep. But only for a little while; then she would lift her head main and say, "So now I can go on again!" And her twofold occupation would begin anew.

When I was thirteen years old [in 1853], my eighteen-year-old sister Bernhardine married the aforementioned

Friends And School

Louis Franke, a lawyer from Germany, who now raised tobacco and manufactured cigars. At that time many people raised tobacco. We did too, for it paid very well.

When my sister moved away with her husband, still more responsibility lay on my shoulders. I had to attend to all of the washing. Our mother was not strong. I also washed for a cigar manufacturer who boarded with us. I took my time with the washing, and it probably was not always so very well done. I also did much of the cooking at the fireplace. Early in the morning I baked the corn bread in our Dutch-oven. The glowing coals were brought out with the tongs, and the oven with the dough inside was set over them, and then more coals were placed on the lid of the oven.

New immigrants came to us, and others; friends and acquaintances when they traveled through the settlement boarded with my parents. Their offers of payment for the meals were never accepted by my parents. Then they frequently gave me fifty cents, probably because they had seen me with a hot face cooking by the fireplace. And I accepted the money, saved it, and bought cows with it. When I married I had twenty-seven head of cattle that I had bought and raised. But to return to our cooking in our home on the Bernard. Yes, we had work there that you children will never have to perform. But there was much that was easier and simpler, e.g., the clothing. The girls of today would turn away if they had to wear the kind of clothing we wore. But our nice Sunday clothing came from our grandmother in Germany. Quite often when relatives and acquaintances came over from Europe, she sent a chest-of-drawers full of cloth and everything one can think of along, from silver-plate to cloth for all kinds of garments, some already sewed. And if the chest-of-drawers was not yet full, she filled all the gaps with dried fruit. Then there were always nice Christmas presents for us, too. When such a chest-of-drawers came, there certainly was great rejoicing. It must also have given our grandmother pleasure to be able to do this for us.

During the Civil War we received letters oftener from her than she from us, and when the war ended, the news came that she had already died.

After the first hard years were over, my parents had asked her to come and live with us, but she had replied that she felt too old.

Now I will insert a few verses that my niece, Frieda Fuchs, dedicated to my grandmother's memory on the occasion of the Fredericksburger celebration for our pioneers of Fredericksburg in particular, and Texas in general. This poem appeared in the celebration issue of the Fredericksburg newspaper in the year 1921.

My Great-Grandmother

Then move to it, the free land,
And seek your fortune there.
It was your wish for many a year,
With wife and children, my dear son.

Not long — my dear old mother,
Not long — and you shall be with us.
When I have sheltering roof for you,
Then you will come, dear Mother, too.

She looked at him with friendly laughter:
And I shall wait till I can come.
In spirit I will go with you,
So that I shall not lonely be.

And many a year has passed away:
Now, Mother, you are welcome,
We have built for you a sheltering roof,
Dear Mother, come to us at last!

How I should like to be with you:
In my new room, o'er there,
With you, my son, with your sweet wife,
To see you there in your new home.

Your children, who are now too big
To sit on Grandmother's lap,
How I should like to see them,
And hear them talk to me.

And yet, my son, forgive me,
It is better now, that I stay.
For I am now infirm and old,
They nurse me here, my son.

Your strength, my only child,
Belongs to your family, over there
In the lovely, new, free land,
Where you now labor with strong hand.

I think of you with happy heart,
And thank God that all's well with you
On all your journeys, Son,
With you there goes your mother's
*   blessing.*

Forget me not in the German land,
In your home at the forest's edge,
Where oak tres stand and violets bloom.
For you I shall always long.

   Now I do not know for certain how long we lived on the Bernard. In all probability it was six years. There another little brother was born [in 1851], and during this period my sister Bernhardine was a great help to our mother. Father said the little brother might be president someday. After that we called him "Dente." When he was older, he protested and always said, "My name is not Dente; my name is Julius." He was the only one of us children to receive more schooling here, and our parents also sent him to Germany for two years' study, so that he should become a good teacher.

He taught for several years at Black Jack and Cypress Mill. At first he was tutor in the home of Eduard Ebeling, where he met his future wife. Father and Ebeling had been boyhood friends in Germany.

Bernhardine and Johannes had already received schooling in Germany. I had also learned the elementary reading and writing, but I forgot it all and had to start over again here with my mother. Our mother taught us children. We also learned much from the talk of our parents and from their conversation with intelligent and educated people, to which we enjoyed listening. What our mother read to us, as well as our own reading of good books, also taught us much. I particularly enjoyed learning history with my mother, and the German language interested me very much.

Brother Bernhard received private instruction in later years. He showed much interest for science and philosophy. He was a real thinker, and as a youth he frequently made all kinds of assertions that later turned out to be scientific facts. Unfortunately, in those first years the means for good and regular schooling were not at hand. Brother Bernhard should have become a teacher.

Brother Johannes was very musical. Sister Ida was our peace-angel, while Lina enjoyed teasing us. Each one, also our ship-baby Friederike, called Rike, was full of a desire for learning that unfortunately could not be satisfied.

Our families, Fuchses and Rombergs, have always visited each other in friendly fashion. The parents thought much of each other, even after we Rombergs moved to Black Jack [in Fayette County] and the Fuchs family moved to the mountains in Burnet County. I always continued to correspond with my childhood friend Ino.

Three Weddings and Departure from the San Bernard

Three weddings took place in our small loghouse: First, our mother's sister, Caroline Bauch, married the Swiss engineer Getulius Kellersberger [January 16, 1851]. (His reminiscences appeared in the *Freie Presse für Texas* not long ago.) Then her sister Louise Bauch married her cousin, Adolf Bauch, although the family tried to dissuade them, as they did not believe in marriages between close relatives. And what followed proved that they were right. The last was the marriage of my sister Bernhardine to Louis Franke. They were married by Rev. Adolf Fuchs [January 20, 1853], and moved to Fayette County, where Franke became an excellent farmer. Later he was elected state representative. In Austin he lost his life in an unexplained way. He was found unconscious at the foot of the steps of the old Capitol on the evening of pay-day [February 20, 1873]. My sister Bernhardine Franke brought up all her children, five sons and two daughters, to be very able people. The youngest was not a year old when his father died.

I think I was thirteen years old when our father sold our place on the Bernard [1853]. He sold it to Andreas F. Trenckmann, the father of W. H. Trenckmann, who is known to us and many other Germans as the publisher of the *Austin Wochenblatt*, but who at that time had not yet been born. Now I shall share something with you that I wrote in the year 1856: reminiscences of our departure from the Bernard. It was a contribution to our *Prairie Blume* (Prairie Flower), a small literary society which we had organized with our neighbors in Black Jack, the Perlitzes in particular.

Old Remembrances

I can still clearly see our former farm [on the Bernard], with the low log-house with the gray oak-shingled roof. And I could not dispute it, if someone asserted that the house with the mellowed spots and the yellow clay-daubed logs by no means looked beautiful.

Nevertheless, it had its good points; for it was very warm, and in the winter when the north wind howled, and, with his voice that made one shudder, went through the tree tops and whipped them about until they broke, and fell crashing to the ground, then it was very cozy within. For as soon as we had eaten supper, the large settee was pushed before the fireplace, another log put on the fire, and we all sat down before it in a half circle, and pleasant conversation shortened the evening for us. Often anecdotes and ghost stories were told. But the greatest pleasure for us children was when Father told us a story. Then we sat quieter than the mice that often attracted our attention with their squeaking and scampering. We followed with close attention the heroic deeds and adventures of a young knight. But it seemed very cruel to us that Father often left the hero in great danger, lying under a tree, knocked unconscious by his enemies, and almost covered with ice and snow, and with the greatest cold-bloodedness took a puff on his long pipe, with much pleasure blew out the blue smoke with many pauses between puffs, and then, after a long pause, as though he wanted our impatience and the warm sympathy that we felt of the hero to cool off first, continued with the story. In this manner the evening soon passed away, and the admonition to go to bed always came too early to suit us. But as soon as we were in our beds and had pulled the coverlet over our heads, after we had listened a few minutes to the struggle of the north wind with the large tree beside our house, whose branches, moved by the wind, often hit the roof, we went to sleep.

When we moved to the farm, on one side of our house there was originally a thicket of trees, underbrush, and grape vines. Here we went one Sunday with hoes and spades, and before the sun went down, after four hours of work, where there had been only brush and weeds there was now a nice roomy arbor, so thickly covered with grape vines that the sunlight could not come through. Before it a large round flower bed had been made and in the center of the bed stood a cactus plant with many small sharp thorns, surrounded by prairie flowers. To our dismay the cactus unashamedly and with great conceit spread out and with great perseverance crowded out almost everything else. The arbor was soon improved by the addition of a table and a bench. Here we all drank our coffee on Sundays, and our parents talked away the afternoon with our neighbors. On work days, during the noon rest-hour, this was the playground for us children. We did not sit down sensibly to read; no, we played tag, and that even in the trees, while we climbed on the vines from one tree to another, and screamed, laughed, and were as happy as children can be.

As soon as we were tired of this play, I called to my brother Bernhard, and in a few minutes, with me leading, we were up in a large tree, also overgrown with grape vines, which stood in the peach orchard, and we looked out of the topmost branch of the tree. Oh, but it was

nice there; I could look far over our field to our neighbors' place and here and there see someone already going to the field. I looked down at our house; it looked so small and unimportant.

Then I turned my eyes to the north, where the Bernard with its white, sandy bottom flowed close by; on its bank the dark green live-oaks grew, and many of these could say: "Here on my trunk she has also often climbed up with her brother and sat on the gnarled branches and whistled all kinds of melodies."

The thick shade of the vine-hung tree that stood on the north side of our house did us little good, for here resided His Excellency the big, magnificent rooster, with the red double comb, the sharp spurs, and the long, drooping tail feathers, as unlimited ruler, very despotic over his little monarchy that had about one hundred subjects, with whom, however, he knew how to get on in a very friendly way.

In the early morning he flapped his strong wings together, and cried in a voice that could be heard at a great distance "Cook-a-doodle-doo!" which meant as much as "Children, wake up!" The space under this tree I should like to call the Harem of the Longnecks, for here the great gander, surrounded by all his flock, sat the whole night and talked, moving his head and neck politely to and fro with great eloquence. And with his neck far outstretched he turned from one goose to the other with his hoarse, snorting voice.

The geese then gave their assent by a modest shake of the head or a low agreement to his snorting. In the evening when I sauntered around the house and saw the old ruler, how with great dignity he again dished up some old story, I would stand still a minute and listen to his gabbling. But as I could not understand any of his speech, it gave me pleasure to jump suddenly between him and his companions, so that they were startled and ran off in all directions. But then, as soon as he had recovered from his first fright, he began with a loud voice to reproach me for my mischievous behavior, and I tried to reply in his own language, while I also moved my head and neck and imitated his steamboat-like snorting. But as we could not come to an understanding, I would give another jump and run away.

It was a clear, warm summer evening, and after a full day's work we were sitting with our friends and neighbors on the south side of the house, on the "moonlight-bench" which always stood under the tall, slender poplar which Father had planted five year before, under whose branches of rustling leaves we had for several years spent our summer evenings in the company of our friends. Today we were sitting there again, and again were enjoying the rustling of the leaves and the bright full-moon that was just rising in the east and looking kindly at us through the trees. But it was the last time that we sat here, for our farm had been sold; already it belonged to another, and early tomorrow morning we were to leave the place, as well as our nice cattle, and every object of which we had pleasant memories, and again accustom ourselves to something new and strange. I stood up and went to the arbor to bid it farewell again; it had aged in the last six years, for in many places the moon looked through the branches and the vines and changed the dark shade to twilight. A ray of the moon showed me the old bench and table, on which time had also laid its hand, for in places they were decayed. Beetles and worms had gnawed and perforated the old wood. I said, "Farewell, you old friendly playground, for we are seeing each other .for the last time." And that was true, for the new owner cut it down, and the green vines on which we had swung have now rotted.

As I went back, past the large tree, someone snorted at me and startled me so that I jumped back. "So, it is you, old comrade," I said, as I saw the old gander, who with turkey-red, high-held head earnestly looked at me. Then after a pause he stretched out his head towards me and poured out a volley of words in his language: "Yes, we must also bid each other farewell and we shall never meet again—never, never! Oh, that is a hard word, and I tell you frankly that I am sorry, even if we have always quarreled, and could not endure each other. In spite of that we were always good friends and therefore I am giving you a sincere farewell!" I then asked the proud ruler of the tree to wake me early in the morning for the last time; and then I went back to the company, who were singing, as we had done so often in the evenings. After all the acquaintances had given us their hands in farewell and had expressed the hope that the new farm would please us and had left us, we went in to rest, so that we could start on our journey with new strength on the morrow.

On the Navidad

We went for a short stay with our sister and brother-in-law Franke, and also to the old Perlitzes, who had offered us a home, till Father bought a place five miles away on the Navidad at Black Jack Springs.

At that time only Americans were living there, until our brother-in-law Franke also moved there, and our farms lay side by side.

The Americans were good, kind people, but they had very little culture, and that explains why we children did not attend their school and were so unfamiliar with the English language. In the beginning we visited them. The women sat before the fireplace, smoked corncob pipes, and spat into the fire; that did not tempt us to become better acquainted with them. At their invitation I went to their singing on Sunday; it was no pleasure! And yet it may have been wrong to draw back coldly from them. My brothers later went to their school, but I preferred to study German at home with Mother and took great pains and said to her, "I'll try at least to learn to write a German letter."

How glad we were to find a good house on this place. It was also a log-house, but built of nice "bottom cedar" logs, well hewn without bark. It did not take long till we had a good orchard here, for the soil was very rich and productive.

Only a few miles to the east of our farm lived the [Friedrich] Perlitz family, and from there to the little town of La Grange stretched the Latin Settlement, so-called since go many well-educated people lived there, even several nobles, who, not being conceited, tried to learn to make a living for themselves and their families. Here we were drawn on Sundays. With the Perlitz family, particularly, we were soon on friendly terms, for their children, Carl, Anna, Lina and Werner, were of our age. To this family we owe many happy hours. Later we young people of the settlement formed a literary society, "Prairie Flower." We contributed little essays and read them aloud, after which there were refreshments, dancing, and games. We also often played charades there, which gave pleasure and exercised the memory. But that was not easy for the girls who had dressed themselves up fine. They stood back then, but it gave me pleasure and I did my best.

My brother Johannes was my escort and good comrade. He was always in good spirits. Half of his life was spent in singing. I can still see him as he went to the field standing on old Hans's broad back and singing with all his might. He sang wherever he was and whatever he did; even when he came home at midnight I heard him singing his songs far off. Later he was president of the singing society in Schulenburg, where he had moved when he could not farm any more; and he died the night after an evening during which he had taken part in a singing program.

Also sister Caroline, called Lina, sang much as a child. Cousin Adolf Bauch often said, "Lina will be a singer!" My sisters Ida, Lina, and Friederike, all three enjoyed singing, and later on our brother-in-law Louis Franke taught them songs, which they all enjoyed very much.

All of this made our week's work lighter. And how nice it was for us, when we and the Perlitz children were frequently allowed to visit each other during the week. Anna Perlitz was several years older than I, very clever and well read. She and Mother often enjoyed a talk. Lina Perlitz (Caroline Perlitz) was pretty much the same age as my three younger sisters, and when she was staying with us she went with us to the fields every time to chop. Then there was much fun and talking! I also had to tell them stories, to which they listened with interest. Sister Lina sometimes gave "lectures" — comical ones — at which we others laughed, or "instructive" ones. You perhaps think, "They probably forgot to chop!" No, the chopping was done; I saw to that!

Later on it was usually Brother Bernhard and Lina Perlitz who were deep in conversation about all kinds of things. After the Civil War they were married. What rarely happens here came to pass: Out of their childhood friendship grew a youthful affection and love that lasted all their lives. But alas! on July 18, 1914, she had to leave him behind, as she, so early, had to depart from this life.

But to return to our childhood, in which we knew so many different ways to lighten our field work. In the black soil not only what was planted grew well, but also all kinds of rank weeds, e.g., the wild morning-glories, which in full bloom made a lovely picture in the early morning. But they also had to be exterminated, like so many others.

When I came out of the field at noon, hot, I liked to take a bath in the bath-house by the well in the garden, which was very refreshing to me. Mother warned me, "I do not think that is good; you are still too hot and the water is too cold!" "Oh, Mother, there is nothing better!" I replied.

But I soon noticed that it was not good for me, and I became sick. Never before nor since have I been so sick. Let this be a warning to you: Never bathe when you are hot!

When I was recovering again, a several weeks' stay at the Perlitzes' did me good.

During the first years that we lived on the Navidad, my sisters Ida, Lina, and Friederike (called Rike) were too young to help continuously in the field. They had a splendid playground outdoors, under the trees. Each built herself a doll house on a "selected site." Lina and Rike chose wood as a building material. Ida, on the other hand, built hers from stone. Each doll house was then provided with furniture, curtains, etc. Then there were doll parties, first at one doll house and then at another. One time Mother's mother came to us with a large dish full of dolls which she had found: "Now just look at this!" — Perhaps the dish was a "wagon," naturally pulled by oxen, in which the dolls were visiting. For at that time in Texas there was no other way of traveling. Oh, how slowly such a wagon went from place to place! But that kind of traveling also had its fine points: If you saw some especially beautiful flowers growing beside the road, you jumped off and picked them, and then easily caught up with the slowly moving wagon. And when you arrived at your destination, the flowers could be given to the dear aunt. To be sure, it sometimes happened that they had withered by that time.

My brother Bernhard used his free time to make all kinds of experiments or attempts. At one time he wanted to become a painter; at another time he made an hour glass. Then he tried to do sculpture in the nice white sandstone that you could find near the Navidad. Sister Rike had to sit as his model. He managed to make a pretty good face. For a long time Father called the rather large bust "Bernhard's idol."

Lina Perlitz showed interest in and comprehension of Bernhard's attempts and experiments. Often they had long discussions and conversations. When these seemed too long and earnest for my sister Lina, she frequently dressed herself as a boy and appeared so on the scene with the introductory words, "I am Mr. Schniepel!" Then she gave more or less comical lectures, in order to break up their conversation. The result was that Lina laughed heartily and Bernhard was a little out of humor. This caused sister Lina to talk still more; she always enjoyed

On The Navidad

teasing when she was a child. Even now, in her old age, she frequently shows her delight in teasing, although life has made her earnest. Her husband, brother-in-law Hermann Fuchs, suffered very much from headaches, and she had two sickly children, Frieda and Albano, who through her careful nursing finally gained strength, however. All were glad that the third child, Johanna, was strong.

We children usually spoke the Mecklenburger "Plattdeutsch" [Low German] to each other. As we grew older, it was only with trouble and will-power that we learned to speak High German to each other. We had always done so in talking, to our parents, although my father himself sometimes enjoyed talking "Platt" with some Mecklenburger friend, e.g., with Rev. Adolf Fuchs. We children always especially enjoyed listening to a conversation in "platt."

Here are a few samples of Sister Lina's teasing: In our bedroom was a cedar beam, and Lina made the discovery that if she struck it with her fist it gave out a peculiar thundering sound. That was just the thing for her. Consequently, one evening on a clear day she beat on it very skillfully. It did not take long before we heard Father say, "It is thundering! Where is the thunderstorm?", and he went out and looked up at the sky in all directions. Little by little the carefully kept secret was discovered, and when it thundered, Father would say, "Is that thunder? Or is Lina drumming on the beam again?"

At another time she imitated the humming of an insect under the window where Mother was reading aloud to Father. At last Father said, "Where is that old animal?" The "insect" was still. As the reading began again, the insect "came" nearer and nearer; she understood how to imitate the sound with her lips. Father again came forward; "There is that old animal back already!" and wanted to look at it more closely; but there was no more of it to be seen or heard. As this humming was frequently heard, Lina was finally discovered to be "the humming insect." She often played similar tricks.

Our youngest brother, Julius, also liked to tease. He even teased our dog, with whom he played "Hide-and-go-seek," while he ran with him around the house and through the hall which joined the two log rooms. The dog looked for him until he found him. That game also pleased John Wenmohs, whose parents had moved into our neighborhood, and the two boys and the dog had many happy games together. Father then laughed and said, "Yes, boys and dogs belong together!"

The [Adolf] Wenmohs family lived about a mile from us. Brother Johannes and I often went there in the evening, after the day's work was done, and talked for hours.

In the summer evenings we frequently sat with our parents in front of the house under the sky, and they taught us the constellations or talked of world events. One time my mother said, "Germany will yet become a republic! We shall not live to see it, but you children may. And then think of us!"

And I did think of my parents when Germany became a republic nine years ago [in 1919] — seventy-one years after they left Germany in order to let their children grow up in the freedom of a republic.

Travels by Horse and Wagon

It was a happy event [Christmas time, 1858] when my friend Ino with her sister Ottilie and her father Rev. Adolf Fuchs came from the mountains to visit us. She also stayed with us when her father and Ottilie traveled on to their old home at Cat Spring; and we lived through happy days, till her father and sister came for her on their return home.

Later I went on horseback with my father and Uncle Hermann Bauch to the mountains, to visit Ino Fuchs; she was very lonely there and always wrote such longing letters, asking me to come and visit her. So it came about that I made the journey with my father and uncle when they went to look at the mountain region with the idea that if they found a place which pleased them, they would move there. But nothing came of that.

At that time the region was so thinly settled that it was hard to find your way. Until we got to Austin it was easy, but then we crossed back and forth. Nowhere could we find settlers of whom to inquire our way, and it was very fatiguing. Finally on the fourth day we came to the old [Jessie] Burnam place [on Double Horn Creek]. There from the heights we saw, in the twilight, the water of the Colorado River as far as down to the Falls and saw the full-moon illuminating the region. And at the foot of the mountain [Castle Mountain] the dogs were barking at Turners' place, neighbors of the Fuchs family, whose residence was in the valley near the river. It was a glorious picture and a comfortable feeling to know that we would soon, after a tiresome journey, be greeted by our friends.

Here I shall insert a poem of my father, Johannes Romberg's:

On the Colorado River

The river rushes o'er the rocks,
It roars the whole night long.
To the sound I fell asleep,
And woke to hear its song.

How many thousand years have fled,
Since first it foamed upon the rock;
How many other men, perhaps,
Have dreamed beside its waves!

And many thousand years again will pass,
Fast as a summer day,
Another then may stand upon this bank
And watch these sparkling waves.

And as it flows from place to place,
So also flows swift Time,
Unceasing and without a pause,
Into the ocean of eternity.

Now every day we went on an excursion, the Castle Mountain, or to a vigorous, bubbling spring where we ate our lunch. As the days were hot, we made use of the moonlight nights, and when we came home late, we looked through Mother's cupboard to still the hunger that our rambling had given us. We were up early the next morning to take a boat ride to the Falls, where the town of Marble Falls now stands.

I had to go with "Willie." He had a long, small boat, hewn out of a tree trunk; only two people could sit in it, in each end one person and between us the luggage — quilts and the provisions. The others all sat in the large family boat. When we arrived at our destination, we climbed and jumped about to view everything before the sun got too hot. It came naturally, that we, Willie and I, were much together. It also happened that Willie was the first to greet us when we finally arrived at the Fuchses', after our long ride in the mountains. I never forgot that. On our excursion on the Colorado it did not take long to catch more fish than we could eat. The men took charge of frying them, while we girls watched and then helped to eat them.

Here I will tell you children that later, when Wilhelm, called "Willie," the second son of Rev. Fuchs, was my husband, for weeks here at Marble Falls, he made powder for the secessionists during the Civil War.

On our return home, Conrad, Ino, and Willie accompanied us as far as Hammit Cave, to look at it with us.

My father gave expression to his memories of this trip into the mountains in the following poem:

Remembrance

Dreams do not tease me!
I have ended the journey,
I have seen the mountains;
Under the hospitable roof
Of a friend I have rested
And passed happy hours.
And guided by friends
Have climbed to Castle Mountain's
    summit
And looked into the distance.
Packsaddle's form, so seldom seen,
Reared itself far to the west,
Surrounded by the fragrant azure,
The cedar dark and evergreen
Their summits circling,
To east and west high peaks
Towered aloft in various shapes.
See, out of the valleys upward,
A pleasant sight now greets our eyes.
Northward up the valley winds
The giant serpent of the river.

Has the gentle water, woman-like
Softly cut this path in granite,
Slowly filled it through the ages?
Or is it like a man
Who walks with force and devastation
Headstrong on his way,
Crushing all that lies before his path?

But I am standing at the grotto's
Gloomy entrance,
Night is near,
And I am seized with shudders.
Totters there the rock?
It hangs down dark with threats!
And the evil force of demons
Moves to hurl the cliffs.
But how different in the morning sun
I see this chasm wild.
Two pillars tall of stalagmite
Bear the grotto's arch erect;
High from the cornice hangs
The moss and lush, green vines
Unmoved by breath of air,
By trickling water cooled.
Light fills the grotto,
Glows back from walls of rock.
Water, pure as crystal,
Clear like mirror, offers
Boon unto the thirsty,
From a bowl of marble.
But the nymph of the grotto,
Where tarries she?
Coarse hands have shattered
Erstwhile beauties of the cave
Mid savage roaring,
Then she fled away forever.
Alas, she sits among the rocks end
    weeps!
She weeps, till tears at last do soften
And penetrate the stony marble.

But now I have returned,
The land I journeyed through,
A rich, romantic picture, Still lies within
  my memory.
Shall e'er I see you after,
And shall I once again
Beneath that cordial roof,
Greet those merry, cheerful friends?

Calm Nature was peaceful,
The country was glorious in sunlight,
Friendly it spoke to me,
Like the whisper of poplar leaves.
I should like to understand it,
When it speaks in thunderstorms.
When it writes hieroglyphics
With the lightning on the gloomy clouds,
And the mountain tops enkindle
In the sudden quivering light.
And when the thunder's crash
Re-echoes from the trembling mountains,
And with hoarse bellows rolls
From valley unto valley;
When down the mountainsides
Boisterous torrents run,
But Nature, she is always
The loving Mother to us.
Whether from lofty clouds her quivering
Lightning comes, to crush us,
Or flower scent is blown to us
In budding springtime.
The human heart is fickle
And alters soon its sentiment.
Loving Mother Nature!
So he calls in ecstasy,
When Day, in thoughtful mood,
With glorious hours has blest his course.
But when beneath man's feet
The firm earth quakes

And Vulcan's fiery outburst
With lava devastates the earth,
Then quakes he in his heart,
Trembles in fear and terror.
But Thou Eternal yet art always
The loving Mother of us all.
Whether Thou with mighty hand
Crumblest the wandering stars
Or paintest the peach's down
With lovely color.
In Thee there moves a spirit,
A living thought flows through Thee,
That mind of man still fails to grasp,
But which the loving heart does trust;
For in the human heart itself
Abides the loving soul of Nature.

This same year (September, 1859), Brother Johannes and Carl Perlitz made a journey on horseback "to the mountains" to the Fuchses', to help celebrate the wedding of Tilie Fuchs and Carl Goeth. Tilie was already engaged when I was there with my father and my uncle. Her bridegroom had just visited her. We met him about ten miles from the Fuchses', as he was returning home. We knew of Tilie's engagement, and, although we had never seen him before, we recognized him as her bridegroom, for he wore a red rose on his white straw hat. Besides, it was a rarity to meet anyone in that almost unsettled region.

In the following year I made still another journey to the mountains and this time at the wish of Anna Perlitz, who wished me to accompany her there; we went with my father and Kellersberger. Uncle and Aunt Kellersberger were visiting us with their small children, after he had made surveys in California and several other states.

He wished to visit the Fuchses in their new mountain home. Again many excursions were made, on which

Willie and I were almost always together, and Conrad, the Fuchses' oldest son, and Anna Perlitz. Later Anna said to me that it was painful to her that she and Conrad usually walked or rode silently together, while Willie and I always had something to talk and joke about.

On other occasions it was so easy for Anna to be entertaining. I wonder whether that was already a sign that their natures did not harmonize, in spite of their love for each other—as was shown in their later marriage?

Unfortunately, neither one became happy.

When Wilhelm visited me later, it was just the time before the war with its stirring sentiments for or against the North—or slavery—and it impressed me very much how freely and with what spirit Willie spoke of Lincoln.

Engagements and Weddings

As far as I know, I am the only one of the sisters whose engagement came to pass in a romantic way. Of Bernhardine's engagement I do not know anything exact, only that the engagement was celebrated in the evening in our arbor on the shores of the Bernard, with lights in the trees, and that it was very romantic and festive. With Willie and me the engagement came about in the following way: I was busy with my favorites, my flowers. Towards evening a norther blew up, and there was a debate whether there would be a frost in the morning or not, whether it was necessary to cover the flowers. Wilhelm, who was intending to leave for home the following day, was of the opinion that it would freeze. I looked for sacks to cover the flowers. When I came carrying them into the garden, where my favorites stood, Willie was already there, and over the flower bed we extended our hands to each other for life. — But nevertheless Willie went home the next morning, for Mother was so "cruel" as to say, "He wanted to go, and now he shall go!" — Whether it froze the next morning or not I cannot recall.

Ida, my next oldest sister, never married; she was still comparatively young when she liked to be called "Aunt Ida" by everyone, and we sisters could listen without envy when she was praised: "There isn't a better aunt in this world." Her small nieces and nephews not only thought highly of her then; they still did when they grew up. Everyone who came in contact with her felt love and esteem for her. How often she was our "good angel" in time of sickness! Through her faithful nursing more than one life was saved. She will not be forgotten; neither has she lived in vain! We are perhaps at this time particularly sensible of that since on February 26, 1926, she softly went to sleep, without long suffering. "A more beautiful death one could not have wished for our good sister!" was the utterance of Sister Rike.

But in this section I intended to tell about engagements. Sister Lina had just cut a large basketful of fresh, green rye, with which she intended to feed the milk cows, when Brother-in-law Hermann came to her with a letter, containing the fateful question, which he then repeated orally after he had taken the large basket from her. He received a satisfactory answer to his proposal. — Later at supper the bridal pair, especially the shy Lina, was teased, and someone remarked that it was surprising that she had had the courage to become engaged. Then Lina answered, "But what else could I do? He had already taken away my basket;"

That was six years after my marriage, and the hard war years were just over. The period of Lina's engagement was also a difficult time, for she caught yellow fever, which at that time raged in La Grange, and it was two years before she had fully recovered from it.

Sister Rike's engagement to Carl Perlitz came to pass while she was feeding the chickens. That was during Lina's engagement, and the sisters' wedding was at first planned for the same day, July 10, 1869. But Carl Perlitz's mother wished that the sisters would not marry on the same day, and Rev. Fuchs was willing to marry Rike and Carl Perlitz one day earlier, although he had already prepared one wedding sermon for both couples. On July 10, Rev. Fuchs gave his festive wedding sermon, and the main celebration was on that occasion, which was also Father and Mother Fuchs' wedding day. Lina Perlitz was at that time already our sister-in-law, for Bernhard and she became engaged after the return home of my two oldest brothers, who with Carl Perlitz and many other friends and acquaintance had left the country so they would not have to fight against their convictions in the

Engagements And Weddings

Civil War. Johannes met and won his wife much later. She was Caroline Bühring from Germany, a music teacher. She had a fine voice, and he and she sang many songs to her accompaniment.

But to return to October 8, 1861, when my Wilhelm and I married. That was at the beginning of the war, and my brothers were still at home. Tilie and Carl Goeth came from New Ulm for our wedding. My dear childhood playmate Ino came with her father. Conrad Fuchs and Anna Perlitz had married several weeks before and already lived in the mountains. — I still remember the thought that Rev. Fuchs expressed in his wedding sermon: he said that in hard times it was especially necessary to protect the family, and in developing this theme he referred to Goethe's Hermann and Dorothea. (This book as well as the other works of Goethe we received as a wedding present from Brother-in-law Franke.) I was happy to have all my brothers and sisters present on that day, as well as other relatives and my mother's mother, who lived with us, a very capable, practical woman.

To give you children an insight into the conditions at that time, I will mention that Wilhelm wanted to be married in a coat that was outwardly still to a certain extent presentable, but the lining of which was slit to pieces. But at my request he went to the nearest store and bought himself a new coat. He came in a large ox wagon, with four yoke of oxen, and a load of wheat. He brought the wheat for the purpose of selling it at La Grange. With this money we bought a stove and other necessary things for house-keeping, also half a dollar's worth of coffee which had to last all the long, war years.

Before I end this chapter of engagements and marriages, I shall relate to you that our youngest brother, sixteen years after my marriage, also married a friendly, cheerful Lina. Now each of my brothers had both a wife Lina and a sister Lina all his own!

As a teacher in Eduard Ebeling's home, Julius became acquainted with Lina, the daughter of his friend Otto Mackensen. Last year, March 15, 1927, Julius and his Lina, celebrated their golden wedding day in the family circle of beloved and successful children and grandchildren. Each of my three brothers had a faithful and congenial companion in his Lina. And Brother Julius is the most fortunate, for he still has his wife; all of us other brothers and sisters are widowers or widows. Bernhardine followed her long lost Louis Franke in 1918, and "Joline" her Johannes in 1910.

Father, in fun and for the sake of clarity, had rechristened his Lina-daughters-in-law and his daughter Lina by fixing the first syllables of their husbands' names as the first syllables of their own names. So Johannes' wife was called "Joline"; Bernhard's Lina, "Berline"; Julius', "Juline"; and his daughter, "Herline," as Hermann Fuchs' wife. How I must relate an amusing coincidence: each of my sisters-in-law had a sister Anna. In the case of Berline and Juline it was the only sister. Juline's only sister, Anna Mackensen, became the second wife of Wilhelm's youngest brother Bennie (or Benno) in 1894.

After a brief married life with Emma Kellersberger (daughter of my aunt and her husband), Bennie had been left a widower, with two small children who were taken care of by his sisters until he married again. Now, children, shall I also tell of the marriage of the youngest granddaughter of your grandfather and grandmother Rev. Adolf and Luise Rümker Fuchs—of your Uncle Bennie's daughter, Emma Mackensen Fuchs? On May 30, 1927, in the Houston home of her Uncle Louis Mackensen and his wife Helene (daughter of Bernhard and Berline Romberg), and in the presence of her grandfather, the 97-year-old Otto Mackensen (relative of General von Mackensen of World War fame) and of her Uncle Julius and Aunt Juline Romberg. Emma was married to

Edwin Arthur Beelitz, a German immigrant and the adopted child of a niece of Grandfather Otto Mackensen.

Now my thoughts, grandmother-like, have wandered through time and space: from 1861 to 1927. In all those years many people have found each other and many people have had to tell each other farewell. What all does not this span of sixty-six years enfold! How much happiness and how much sorrow they have held for both individuals and the nation. I am reminded of the words of the song that your grandfather Rev. Adolf Fuchs composed:

Love Is A Jewel

Love is a precious gem,
It burns year-out, it burns year-in
And cannot consume itself;
As long as Heaven's alight,
Love glows in human eye,
And is transfigured there.

In love lies the might of Heaven
Victorious o'er death and might,
No storm disturbs its realm.
Tho' hatred fill the world with menace,
Love keeps its steadfast course.
High as the clouds, Love glows.

At many a wedding among the children and grandchildren of Grandfather Fuchs this song was sung.

Now we return to 1861.

To My Home in the Mountains

All my foods and chattels were packed into Wilhelm's wagon, with four or five yoke of oxen hitched to it, and then off we moved to our now home!

We were barely eight or ten miles from home when a norther blew up with rain, which lasted the entire night. I was surprised the next morning that Wilhelm managed to make a fire to cook coffee. After we had eaten, we went on. The slow rain continued all day. On the following day the sky was clear and a fresh north wind blew, which grew stronger. On October 11, we had a mild frost, so that when we arrived in the mountains we saw that the potato vines were blackened by it. A small, pretty, but very wild place, almost surrounded by rocks, was to be our home [on Tiger Creek]; it was like an oasis in the desert. Where our house was to stand, an impenetrable thicket grew. As it was cleared away, a large old live-oak appeared, the thick trunk making a bend before it stretched upward. In the crook Indians had cut steps, to make it easier to climb the tree. The place had apparently been an Indian camp; a little to the front stood several large poplars, under which there was still visible evidence that it had once been the Indians' sleeping place. The wonderful trees had been partially stripped of bark, and the thick bark had been placed in piles and used as beds. We also found drinking vessels made of horn, etc.

Although the place did not lie low, my husband had to dig only a few feet under these poplars to get nice drinking water. On only one side were there a few acres of very rich farm land, or more properly said, garden land. Wilhelm raised cattle, and this small plot was sufficient. We grew large crops of potatoes, which we could make good use of, also fine rye, such as I had never seen before. It grew almost as tall as my head. It was taken to the Mormon Mill on Hamilton Creek, and very nice flour was made from it. At that time many Mormons still lived there.

In front of our house a splendid stream of water went splashing over the rocks. A more romantic place could not easily have been found! It required much work to open an approach from all directions to the site of the house, so thickly stood the trees, bushes, underbrush, and vines. Willie had bought a log-house from his brother-in-law Carl Andreas Matern, who wanted to move to Pecan Creek, so we did not receive our dwelling so very soon. First we built a back \room, in front of which the log-house was to be built later. The brother-in-law had not yet moved. So Willie took a large wagon sheet and stretched it out where the log-house was to be built. We lived for awhile in our romantic Indian home, till the log-house was vacant and had been torn down and again built up with the addition of a chimney. We had fine smooth-hewn logs for our house. For many years we got along with a home-made bench and two chairs, which we received from my parents-in-law. So often I think, "How different, when a young couple settles down nowadays!"

We experienced uneasy days, because during the war the frontier was not guarded very well, and the Indians therefore returned again and paid a visit here and there, stole horses, and killed white persons who got in their way.

I was usually alone at home, because our husbands, Conrad and Willie Fuchs, had, before the war started, brought a large herd of cattle from the lower country in order to take care of them. (My cows were also in the herd). When I was alone all the long days, I frequently went to my sister-in-law Anna, who lived a quarter of a mile away.

Willie often stayed away for days. Then at night at least one member of Willie's family came to stay with me: Ino, Bennie, or Father Fuchs himself. Only twice was I alone. One time a terrible thunder storm came up to prevent the arrival of my protector. The other time I was alone, my oldest son Theodor had a dreadful attack of croup, of which he often suffered. Often when Papa came home late and I heard the noise of his arrival, I shuddered and believed, or feared, that it might be Indians. Then I asked him to whistle when he came, so that I would know whether it was he or Indians.

One time when Ino wanted to visit Anna and me, she came on horseback, setting out early in the morning, as the moon was shining. When Hermann learned from his parents that she had ridden off—he had been busy outside and had not noticed that she had left—he was excited and said, "It is too dangerous to let a girl ride alone now; I am going to follow and see whether she arrived safely." Between their house and the little Castle Mountain Brother-in-law Hermann saw that the track of Ino's horse was blotted by the fresh tracks of many horses. "Indian horses," thought Hermann immediately and followed them, after he had convinced himself that the tracks of Ino's horse continued on in the right path. And he was correct; they were Indians. After he had followed the tracks over the Colorado, Hermann found a discarded Indian saddle, and the rocks on the other side were still moist from the horses' wet feet. But all pursuit that was started after Hermann's report of his observation was in vain. It came out that the Indians had stolen the horses from our neighbors. That Ino got safely past the Indians can be attributed to the circumstance that she sang in a loud, full voice on the way. She said that just there between the mountains she had enjoyed the echo of her song. Indians are said to believe that singers are protected by the "Great Spirit."

All the trees around our house were inhabited by squirrels that fearlessly sat on the branches, looked at me, and talked to me in their language. That amused me. I cannot remember that one of them was ever shot; but we constantly had venison. We also smoked it, and with pecans it tasted fine on bread. Honey was always plentiful. But we did not have sugar, and everything had to be eaten and cooked with honey, and baked with honey, if one wanted cake. Fruit was also preserved with honey. You had to make the best of circumstances. Later a disease started among the deer, and large numbers died.

Coffee you could not get; so all kinds of substitutes were tried, e.g., grape seeds, black persimmon seeds, or roasted potatoes, which we preferred. When we did not have enough potatoes, we roasted the skins.

One variety of tea tree used to grow here, the leaves of which were excellent, but it was not easy to find. Hogs were at first plentiful, but then a drought came and there were no acorns. Neither had we raised any corn. We did not have money with which to buy or order some, because for everything we took to market, we received a mountain of worthless paper money that no one wanted

Two days before Christmas [1862] Theodor was born, and when he was a few weeks old, Wilhelm took Sister Lina to her parents again. She had been with us several months.

When Wilhelm came back, he brought me some nice lard from Mother. Hurrah! That was a treat! We divided it, so that all the nearest relatives received some. The cattle that Conrad and Willie brought up here to take care of died, and I also lost all the cattle that I had acquired. What was left at the end of the war was taken along to

Kansas by people who drove large herds there and sold them for their own profit. Then for many years all unmarked yearlings were killed.

There were very many rattlesnakes about our house. The dogs bayed at them, and made a great noise until I came, screwed up my courage, and beat on the snake, after which the dogs jumped on it and made an end of it.

I then had the satisfaction of hearing Grandfather Fuchs praise me for my bravery, but what else could I have done? I could not let them live! At one time we had a small rock smoke-house; I was in it one day, and as I turned around, I saw a small snake crawling out over the threshold of the door. I let it get out first, you may be sure!

We had fine times on Sundays and holidays when we all assembled at the grandparents', for they always had plenty of fish and venison roast and Grandmother always had something good in addition to that; the best was the coffee for afternoon lunch, even if it was a substitute, and the music that followed it and the stimulating conversation. Ino had a full, rich voice; the younger brother, Hermann, had a clear tenor; all had fine musical talent, and later there was also Sister Lina (Hermann's wife). Grandfather once said with enthusiasm: "We could travel and Five concerts!"—He himself was very musical, and in his youth he sang wonderfully. I must not forget to mention Conrad, who also was full of music. You could hear him singing at his work or while riding.

Only your Papa and I, children, had no talent and were the silent listeners; but your Papa was always ready when it came to story-telling and conversation. Your Papa understood how to give a friendly word to everyone, wherever he came in contact with people. This talent he inherited from his mother, who on account of this characteristic had won admirers, young and old, large and small. Brother-in-law Hermann had inherited, probably from her, a great talent for story-telling. And we find the gift, here and there, among her grandchildren.

The house of my parents-in-law was very hospitable, and many people went in and out. Everyone received musical or mental stimulation. The children also respected their parents very much.

Here I will insert a poem that Hermann Fuchs wrote, after he had married and was living nearly a mile away from us.

The Parents' House

The Colorado flows along,
Where our old home once stood;
There we dwelt together,
For many a long, long year.

There stands, almost decayed,
The dear parental house. It was so dear to
    all of us;
And yet: we went away!

Now the days have vanished
Those of our happy youth
However much we liked it there –
We all have moved away.

To celebrate the finest feasts
To all was welcome given,
Beloved guests with joy were taken
Into this genial home of ours.

The holidays returned again
And often also many guests,
We sang the sweetest melodies
To Father's violin.

> *When I hear now and then,*
> *The river's song, year in, year out,*
> *It sounds like olden music,*
> *In my dear parents' house. —*
>
> *The stream flows past:*
> *So also hastens time,*
> *Which blooms anew eternally*
> *Throughout Infinity.*

Often Wilhelm said he had an inclination to study the violin; his father at the first attempt to teach him lost patience, however, and gave it up. But he gave those grandchildren who showed musical talent their first lessons, and usually after that they went on practicing by themselves, so that they learned some music and in part were able to improve themselves. It was a strain on Father to teach.

But again I have hurried forward too rapidly in my narrative! — Wartime: The men here in the mountains were not pressed into military service as they were in the low lands, whether they wanted to or not; but they were enlisted and placed in companies to protect the frontier from invading Indians. (For this reason I still receive a pension.) Or they had to work for the soldiers, help prepare war supplies, as, for example, the powder they made at the Colorado Falls. Wilhelm as well as his brothers would have been killed as George Hoppe's father, Hans Adolf Hoppe, was if they had not taken part in such occupations.

The brothers had a friend, a boyhood comrade, who in spite of his hatred for the Union-minded still felt friendship for them, and warned them not to stay here longer, or their lives would not be safe.

Then the large ox wagon was packed with the most necessary things and we moved to my parents'. Brother Conrad Fuchs went with us (his family had already for a long time been staying with their relatives), and he found work in Houston. On the way we had the bad luck — which later turned out to be good — to capsize at Shingle Hills, with all our household supplies, even a churn full of honey. But all went well, with only a few scratches and great fright. I stayed with my parents, with Dora and Hanni and Theodor; Papa worked in a hat factory in La Grange and could be with us on Sunday. At first he had to card wool, to make hats for soldiers; when a carding machine was purchased, he had to iron the hats. In the evening when the dogs barked, little Dora would call with joy, "Papa is coming!" That went on the whole winter. With the spring came the end of the war, and we could again return home. During the war years I braided many hats, some of palmetto which we had brought along from the low land, out of Mill Creek and the Brazos bottom, later also of rye straw, which was very good for that purpose. We sold the hats, and so received some money for our most urgent needs. The paper money was soon worthless. Your papa kept himself in clothing by tanning deer leather.

My mother and sisters spun and wove. From them I also received cloth for clothing. When the large spinning wheel turned and loudly hummed, Father said, "That is the secessionists howling!" This homemade cloth was very strong and outlasted the war. Bernhard made several spinning wheels, for us and for the neighbors. He, as well as Johannes, must have inherited the knack for joiner's work from Father. Among Father's grandchildren we also find this gift again. Johannes made several very nice pieces of furniture from the wood of a walnut tree that stood in our yard on the Navidad: a cupboard, a writing desk, a night-table, etc.

Lina also showed much talent for different kinds of hand work. She was particularly skillful in spinning, and during the war she spun the sewing thread. Later, as

Hermann's wife, she spun his mohair, and crocheted and knitted very nice shawls from it. Because Brother-in-law Hermann all his life suffered at times from headaches, Lina helped wherever she could to earn a living for the family. As Hermann during and after the war made saddles, Lina had already made bright leather holsters for pistols, and later with Hermann's help small tumbler dolls out of lilac, with half lead bullets underneath and dressed in fine, bright paper. These "roly-polies" sold very well. She also spun rope of buffalo hair for saddle girts; Hermann helped her to tie it to the saddle ring. With the money they earned they bought some land in Burnet County, on which is located the ever-flowing "Moonlight Spring."

Later, with the children's help, she made many girths of mohair, for which she spun the rope.

During the Civil War she also braided hats. In her old age she took up this occupation again for her amusement, and in addition braided baskets and trays, with which she won various first prizes at the Fredericksburg and Boerne Fairs.

Here I will also tell of Theodor, our oldest son. He showed talent for wood work, and we wanted to send him to San Antonio so he could receive instruction. But he wished to stay at home, unlike some of the other sons, who were anxious to go away and study; but there was always so much work at home that your papa could not do alone, and "ready" money was also lacking—unfortunately!

Back to the war time: When my brothers, Johannes and Bernhard, who were of age, while Julius was not, saw that it was inevitable that they would be drawn into the army, unless they left the country, they decided to go to Mexico and from there to Central America. They found work here and there to keep themselves alive. I remember that they wrote that they had built themselves a small hut; they covered the roof with vines and bushes that they had tied together with reeds, to secure some protection from the frequent rains, and that the vines, showing the fertility of the soil, grew down to the ground, there took root, and then climbed up again. From there they moved on, looking for and finding work. They took everything that was offered them. I remember that one of them got an old clock to running again; they had been asked whether they understood anything about clock repairing. Often they suffered hardships. Then again things went better. They were in all the states of Central America, also in Panama. At last they parted. Brother Johannes had an opportunity, after a severe illness, to go along to California by a ship as silver polisher. In California he went to the Employment Bureau, and was given a job as shepherd. (He had recovered his health on the voyage.) High in the mountains, in solitude, he herded a large flock of sheep for some time. One day when he went to get meal from his meal sack to make his bread, he noticed that it shook from a slight earthquake. It was through letters which the brothers both wrote to Germany that they again learned of each other's whereabouts. While they were still together, Bernhard was once very sick with fever. In order to get away from the unhealthy place, they traveled with a. horse, which Johannes led, while the sick Bernhard rode and was held upright by his brother. Bernhard always begged, "Let me get off and lie down under a tree!" But Johannes would not allow it—for they had no water—and they went on through the wilderness, till they finally came to a highway. Then Brother Johannes said, "So, now you can lie down!" They waited there until someone came who could give them water.

Johannes always found work more easily than Brother Bernhard because when he was asked whether he could do this or that, Johannes always answered,

"Yes!" — But Bernhard would say, "I have not done it before but I will try!" — whereupon he was not taken so quickly.

Brother Bernhard later on also went to California, to Santa Clara. There it did not rain for thirteen months. But there was subsoil moisture. He worked on a farm. Later he would dearly have like to go back to California. When he left, the farmer asked him what he intended to do when he got home. "Marry!" he answered. "Yes, but do you have the girl's promise?" "No!" was the answer, whereupon the farmer expressed his doubt as to whether the girl would still be there. But his Lina, in spite of everything, was still true to him. I remember her eyes always shone when Bernhard was mentioned.

Johannes traveled by ship from California to Nicaragua. He arrived in the evening, or night, and at once asked whether there were any travelers in the locality, whereupon he received the reply, "There is a Carl Perlitz here!" So he looked for him, to accompany him to New York. Otherwise, Carl Perlitz would have missed the ship. In New York they looked for work because their money was spent. From there they also wrote home, and money was sent to them for their journey back to Texas. This meeting of the friends was a happy event for both, as well as the journey home together. How much they had changed in the years of their absence!

My mother wrote the following, and today, after more than sixty years, I am copying it from her letter:

"Yesterday, Sunday afternoon, we had gone to the Wenmohses'; from there we could see all the roads. Late in the afternoon a lady and four man came riding through the pasture. We recognized Lina, the Perlitz brothers, and Krempkau. Concerning the fourth rider, the others said, 'That is not Bernhard.' But Father and I went to meet them, and the strange rider and Lina turned off and came toward us. It was Bernhard. He had come on foot from Alleyton, and that night he had camped four miles from La Grange, and near noon had arrived at the Perlitzes'. It had not been his intention to propose to Lina right away; first he wanted to see whether she still loved him. He must have seen that very soon, and so a long desired wish has been fulfilled for us. That will be real happiness, when Hermann also comes at Easter.

"It is natural that Bernhard of all the travelers has changed the most. We notice how Americanized he has become. It is hard for him to speak German fluently; he always brings in American phrases. But it is getting easier for him already; when he first came to the Perlitzes', it was much more difficult. Werner said it had seemed just too curious to him.

"But that can be understood, as it was the first German that he spoke in one and a half years. Otherwise his ways are quite the same. I am writing this while the bridal pair and Father are visiting the Wenmohses. What all has happened since I started this letter! Oh, Louise, how happy, how blessed I feel! Our sons are both here, and now this engagement, and my Lina so happy to have her Hermann here. That was an Easter celebration! If only you and Wilhelm could also have been here." (April 8, 1867)

When Johannes returned home, your father and I with our three oldest were still there. When Bernhard came, we were already here in the mountains and living again in the little oasis in the "rock desert." I frequently had with me some of the children of the Materns', who now lived on Pecan Creek. She [Ulrike Fuchs Matern] was glad, for she had her small house so full. Especially the oldest, Marie, later Alois Goebel's wife, was often with me, but also Helene, afterwards Julius Kellersberger's wife, two sisters who were very different. Then later when their father, Carl Andreas Matern, had bought the mill on Cypress Creek and after hard work was taken sick and suddenly died, there was great distress, for on Pecan Creek he had a large flock of sheep that his small sons Adolf and Ino herded, in spite of danger from Indians. Matern's wife, Sister-in-law Ulla, could not stay there alone. Besides, she was expecting the birth of her last daughter, Ulli, now Walter Giesecke's wife. So she moved with her children to her parents and lived in a small house that had previously been occupied by different people. We took charge of the two sons, Adolf and Ino, together with the sheep. They had to herd the sheep. Your father built a large sheep shed, getting the shingles in exchange for a shipment of sweet potatoes.

It was a very uncomfortable time, for the Indians still came visiting. But necessity breaks iron! Later we had a herder; but the sheep did not thrive, and many died. Then your father, children, got the idea that he wanted to take over the mill, for the small piece of land on which we lived would not provide for all of us. All my protests that he did not understand anything about mills, did no good. He took over the mill with the land, without knowing how high the debts on it were. For, good-natured as he was, he also wished to assist his unfortunate sister, who had so many children. The actual value he first learned when he met the former owner in Austin, and it was probably somewhat more than he expected.

Carl Goeth and family at that time already lived on Cypress Creek (he was a sheep breeder), and moving into their neighborhood was also an enticement for us.

LIFE AND WORK ON CYPRESS CREEK
1867-1884

Before all this happened, my Wilhelm had wanted to buy and cultivate the land behind the Flatrock, which Walter Giesecke later owned. There life would perhaps have been easier, even if lonelier, for us; for what work and trouble we encountered on Cypress Creek, as well as sickness—malaria and typhoid fever! It was already rumored at that time that the water of Cypress Creek was not healthful; but your papa thought it was not so bad, especially if you got the drinking water from the nice large spring above —where Lechows [Gustav Lechow] now live.—Papa at first went alone and got everything into order. He had hardly ground a few bushels of meal, when a very hard rain came and his frail board dam washed away; and that happened a second time later. He thought after the first time that he had found out how to construct it better, but it again washed away. Then he got us, and all our goods and chattels, and the work was begun still more thoroughly. We had two large rooms with a hall between, and for the time being we had to get along in these, even with the additional presence of various workmen now and then. I now secured a Negro woman to help me; she was a former slave of our neighbor Burnam, and a very faithful and good creature. She had two children; so a small hut had to be built for her. It was very nice to have her, for with several laborers to cook for and all my children to attend to, I could not manage all my work.

One fall almost all the children were more or less sick. The many wild plums that then grew on the Cypress were probably the cause, but not entirely so. The water, and the evaporation from much old driftwood that lay dammed up in piles and rotting, held fast by vines and dense underbrush, was probably very harmful. Our little

Hermann died there; he was such a dear good boy, so industrious, obedient, and clever. A neighbor once said of him, "He will go to Congress; he is so intelligent!" With his little wagon he continually brought me fire wood from the mill, where there was later so much waste. I never had to urge him to work. He was already rejoicing that he would soon be seven, for then be could go to school. And in addition to that he had been promised a new hat. But he did not live to see his seventh birthday!

Your papa also was once very sick, but fortunately his father was with us and could help nurse him. That proved a great consolation to me. Finally, on a Sunday, Grandfather left us, for he believed that the force of the fever was broken, and he had to go back to his "Little Mother", as he so often called her. But after dinner a workman came, whom Papa had hired to take charge of the wood work. (This workman was also probably more skilled in that line than others.) He spoke very urgently with him of the impending work, and when he left us towards night fall, your papa was entirely exhausted and had a terrible fever. He raved all night, and the next morning he lay still and unconscious. This lasted for two days and two nights. Little Willie, at that time almost two years old, was very sick at the same time. I treated him with wet compresses, etc., and he gradually improved.

The third evening Paul Reinke unexpectedly appeared. He had worked for us for years, but as he often had disagreements with the other workmen, Papa had discharged him. In many ways he had been very agreeable: he had taught our two oldest, Dora and Johanna (Hanni), to read and write; on Sundays, and for Christmas he had made all kinds of presents for them and had also bought some. But his irritable and hotheaded nature sometimes brought on difficulties. Now I felt much relieved, however, to have an acquaintance there, one who also knew how to be very helpful. After another night and a day Papa again regained consciousness, and by degrees he recovered and again returned to his work.

From Blanco Papa got a helper, Mr. Kapp, who had himself already run a mill in Blanco and was experienced. The mill was again repaired, the corn mill first of all. We were half starved. We were getting corn meal from Austin, but it was no good. And the high water again and again stopped work on the dam. Cypress Creek looked entirely different then than now.

Papa ordered some books on the subject of mills from the North. Old Giesecke had recommended them. He studied them and experimented. The publisher's name was Lefell; but when questioned by Papa he wrote, "Yes, I am a real German Löffel! (Spoon)." Finally things progressed so far that some corn was ground, and also some boards were sawed. Just then a peddler came who needed some boards for his wagon bed. Papa, gave them to him in exchange for a piece of calico cloth for a dress, and perhaps something else. The children joyfully brought me the piece of cloth. As it was almost time for dear Grandmother's birthday, I said, "We will send her that; then she will see that we have again advanced a step forward!"

And it seemed that it gave her pleasure, for I heard she had said that she intended to make a dress for her burial out of it. But she lived for many years after that, and saw that the old mill finally amounted to something, though only after many more disappointments and privations on my part. The old mill always had to be improved, and that was expensive. To take the place of the large upright saw a circular saw was bought. And the water broke the dam again, and the turbine that was supposed to drive everything disappeared. Then I said to Papa, "Well, we have had enough of the old mill now. Let's start on something different!" But he said, "No, it will work! We will keep on." And then they went and looked below, and found the turbine half buried in the sand. And they again went to work from the beginning. When the dam had washed away still another time, he came to me and said, "I know now how to build the dam so that it will hold." He showed me how the rock slabs had to be placed, slanting against the stream, so that the water, instead of pushing them apart, pressed them together and then flowed over them. (Later when the dam was built at Austin, Papa said, "The way they are building it, it cannot hold"; and he was right: it broke and had to be rebuilt). Consequently, the work was started again. Neighbors and friends came and said, "We want to help build the dam up again," and many, who could not help with the work, said, "We need the mill, and we will contribute our share to the building." One brought a bushel of corn meal, another a sack of wheat, some gave money, even if not much. One day I had to cook dinner for twenty men, without any help; but they all had enough to eat. They came in wagons, with five yoke of oxen, with shovels and picks, to haul rocks and sand. They did a lot of work, so that Papa could afterwards finish the job with his ox wagon and with the help of his regular workmen. And the dam held! — Now came the results of success:

Out of the profits of the mill all the debts could be paid and workmen given their wages.

By and by Papa bought a shingle saw, then a crosscut saw which cut the wood straight through, to determine the length of the shingles. Then the people came and bought building lumber. At that time the train did not come as far as Austin; and, so with the number of settlers increasing, the mill had plenty of market for building lumber. From all sides, from near and far, as far as forty and fifty and more miles away they came to buy and have their corn ground.

Joseph Giger attended to the corn grinding at night, for during the day the mill was used for sawing wood. Later, with the increase of settlers, more cotton was raised, and the sawing had to stop while the cotton was being ginned. Often the wagons stood crowded from the store to the mill; at first we were literally almost overrun. Not only did I have to pull myself together for the constant noon guests, but many people came in the evenings to have their corn ground, and then very often I had to prepare beds for them, even if only on the floor. If I had not had such an uncommonly healthy constitution, I could not have done all that. But it soon got too much for me, and a regular camp cottage was built. The news spread: "There's a mill; work can be obtained there!" And many people got stranded here.

One man wanted to be school teacher. We let him teach for half a day in our house, and then we learned that he was half crazy. While we were having a hard thunder storm he stood himself in front of me and said, "Come, let's dance!" The next day he was sent away.

One shepherd always put food into his coat pocket at the table; and when he went to get the dog feed, he pulled the braids of the girls, who were washing the dishes. Oh! there were so many vexations and difficulties!

Yet the mill also brought to us many agreeable and interesting people—Joseph Giger, for example. Papa and he complemented each other in their work. Papa understood so well how to get along with people, while Giger was so scrupulously accurate in the bookkeeping and later also helped with the mail and in the store.

Rudolf Bius and John Fackland worked awhile for us; they were agreeable men. I sewed each one a suit. [John A.] Martiny was a skillful blacksmith. His wife [L. W. Martini] was a French Alsatian and spoke French, while her husband spoke German, so their little son Willie spoke French, German, and English. For many years now he has been Judge of Blanco County. — [Frederick K.] Fritz Reiner was a very gifted musician, playing the piano with a wonderfully soft touch. He had a predilection for improvising on the piano, and also composed. — George Hoppe in later years was a cartwright there. (The last two named became our sons-in-law). Previously two Beck brothers were employed by us, one of whom made furniture, while the other was a cartwright. Both came from Germany.

Hermann Lungwitz, the gifted artist, came and painted several pictures of the mill. One of them shows a large cypress trunk being sawed, with Shovel Mountain in the background. Daughter Louise told me that she and some of her brothers and sisters used to walk in a roundabout way down Cypress Creek to the mill, to buy candy from the store with buttons (as money) and then on to where the painter was, to look over his shoulder and watch his work of creating in colors. Out of Mother's sight, to escape many a little task at home — children's tricks and childish pursuits!

Unfortunately we could not afford to buy a picture of the mill. So I was very much interested when after many years I saw one of those pictures in the Nimitz Hotel in the possession of Elise Lungwitz. — Inspired by this incident, Niece Frieda Fuchs wrote the following:

Picture of the Mill

Before a picture of a mill they stand:
Long the pair of aging sisters gaze
And stand beside the daughters also gray.
Again they see the swinging, mill-wheel
   turn
There on the Cypress, many summers gone.

Many a mighty cypress tree

Was shaped and hewn for settler's use,
Those homes atop the hills and on the leas
Wrought from dear dreams of hearth and
    love,
Yet shelter us 'gainst ice and storm.

Here came the lonely settler from afar,
Astride his horse or with his laden ox-cart,
To grind his daily bread. Rough the trails
And slow the way and weary was the labor.
Night and day the mill toiled on and on.

That robust hand which built the mill,
Thus built warm dwellings in the wild,
Has long since rested from its toil.
As well the artist's hand. And yet,
The work of both lives on.

Before the picture of the mill they stand.
Long the pair of aging sisters gaze.
Again they see the singing mill-wheel turn,
There on the Cypress, years on years ago.

Wilhelm, your father, sawed some walnut boards and let them dry, for the purpose of having furniture made from them. While I was staying with Sister Lina and Brother-in-law Hermann to recover after our little Hermann's death and the serious sickness of the other children, the Beck brothers came and your papa had them make me some beautiful furniture, to surprise me with on my return home. After that many of the neighbors came to have wagons and furniture made by the skillful Becks, who had received their training in Germany. Now with such nice furniture, in which so much could be stored, it was much easier for me to keep everything in order. But it was long before I could forget the grief and trouble of the past weeks and months. Some months previous to Hermann's death we had lost a little son as a baby [Paul, born June 17, 1877]. And I am sure that the sorrow and my over-exertion during the long illness of my family was the cause of our Paula's never being a quite healthy child. A pretty baby, with long curls, she almost always lay with open eyes and slept very little. All her life she possessed a dreamy nature; although many school tasks were easy for her and she had a good memory for literature, she lacked the ability to plan her daily work and accomplish it. In spite of that she wished to help and be of use. She had talent for handwork and crocheted many center-pieces and bed-spreads. And when a clock or a machine was out of order, she always very soon found the defect. She had appreciation for beauty and liked birds, flowers, and small children. And yet she was to be pitied. After she had typhoid fever, she became weaker and weaker and died in 1921. I wrote this because I am convinced that a mother's physical, as well as mental and emotional, condition before her child is born does leave an impression on the baby.

In the first years after this region was settled, there were no doctors here, and therefore we treated our children with the "water cure" ("Wasserkur" or hydrotherapy). I still to this day believe in its effectiveness, though it must be used with discretion because of the danger of catching a cold from drafts or from sudden cooling or heating. Nevertheless, I also believe in good doctors. A change of climate also sometimes does wonders, especially with malaria.

Alois Goebel was at that time very friendly and took several of our children to Shovel Mountain, his home, to convalesce. This surely helped them very much. The children really were all sick at this time except Dora, who was in the lower country with her grandmother Romberg, and Theodor, whom we had sent away to a good neighbor, and who therefore kept well.

Papa gradually bought more and more land—after he had paid for the mill and the land that went with it—so that he became the owner of much land between the Cypress Creek and the Pedernales. But all this land and the debts depressed me; I would much rather have had less land and no debts. I did not like to indulge myself in anything, and still I would have liked to have had various improvements in the house and yard. I inherited that from my father; he did not want to have anything that he could not pay for.

So I very, very often stayed at home, when I really would have liked going somewhere. We were invited to Hermann Richter's house and to [August] Schroeter's wedding, and I would have liked to go, but I had to give it up, for I had not the proper clothes. And with all the children it was difficult to go out; so it was best to stay home. Now and again we went to visit our old parents on the river. The Goeths occasionally took us along, also to my brother-in-law and sister, Hermann and Lina, who lived on Tiger Creek. But my main contact was with my sister-in-law, Ottilie Goeth. And their children and ours, who were of about the same age, played much with one another. But it was very difficult then just to get across Cypress Creek, for it had much more water in it those days than it does now. On those visits we sat comfortably together and talked while we did handwork. It was not embroidery, no, usually mending and darning! Tilie and I often talked about training the children, which of course was especially interesting to us. One week she would come to me after dinner, and the following week I would go to her.

After the mill had performed its good service, I also received a sewing machine. At that time it cost a hundred dollars! I then sewed a great deal for the workmen, also for others, to get back the money paid for the good Singer sewing machine, although I really had enough work already, with the many children and the large household. Nothing was bought ready-made; everything had to be sewed, even the men's clothing. No one would think of sewing that now! We did not can foods then so much, however.

In various little houses around us people lived, who found employment with us, like the Beck brothers, for example, and a blacksmith, also from Germany. When one left, another came. So there were always people who wanted to have something sewed, and they could buy the cloth in the little store that Papa had built, which was first managed by Kapp.

In later years Julius Kellersberger (son of the engineer) took over the store, till the nice water in the creek gave out more and more, and the successors had to operate with steam.

In the year 1882, our second oldest daughter, Johanna, married George Hoppe, who was cartwright near the mill. He also often helped build and made very accurate, exact cabinet-work. At first they lived near Cypress Creek below the mill; later, in 1884, they moved four miles above on a farm and ranch. Their oldest son died here on Cypress Creek, and the oldest daughter died at the new home; after that they had four healthy children. Here I would like to mention that Johanna, like her father, always had something kind and cheerful to say to everyone. She suffered a great deal herself, and always had great sympathy for other sufferers and understood how to make them happy. She also never forgot the birthday of a relative or friend, young or old. She was often teased with that, that she knew all the birthdays by heart: "When does this one or that one have a birthday? Only ask Hanni; she can tell you!"

The Hoppes made one nice trip with their little daughter Bertha to the World's Exposition in Chicago. In the year 1897, George Hoppe went to Germany to take over the estate of his uncle, who was an artist. At that time he visited relatives in Hannover, where his daughter, Bertha, later also had a fine time, when she went to Germany in the year 1910. On her return she traveled through New York and Chicago.

The Hoppes bought more land and built themselves a nice home, which he knew how to keep in good condition inside and out.

On this place the youngest son Edwin now lives with his wife Viola, born Herbert; they are taking good care of the place. When the only daughter married, they moved to Marble Falls to give the two younger sons better school opportunities.

The two oldest sons graduated from A. & M. College as engineers; Roland marred Ethel Smith, a teacher from Arkansas. They live in Oklahoma and visited us this summer with a cheerful little son.

Adolf now lives in Georgia with his wife Maria, born Henneberger, of Pennsylvania.

After a brief marriage their daughter Bertha lost her husband Walter Richter [1883-1916] in an unfortunate accident; her parents then went to live with her. Since the death of her mother, her father has been her faithful support and protector.

Her daughter and son, Esther and Walter, Jr., have been attending school in Marble Falls for several years.

Our Home Near the Pedernales

In the year 1884 Papa sold the mill and the land that went with it, and we moved about three miles away to our place near the Pedernales, where our shepherds and their families had already lived many years. Here was a wonderful spring, and as long as that good water lasted, we were all well, for which I was very thankful. Then when dry years came and the spring dried up more and more, our health was no longer so good. Now my son Adolf has owned the place for many years, and has long had a good well with a windmill.

Although our house was not arranged as nicely as I would have liked, we spent many happy hours there. The family alone, when seated at the table, made quite a party. Our meals were frequently eaten to the accompaniment of Papa's droll stories, while the children made remarks or listened with interest. Reinhold, especially always listened attentively.

Our youngest, Johannes, was born in this place. The four oldest, Dora, Johanna, Theodor, and Willie, were born in the "Oasis of the Rock-Desert." The other children all came into the world on the banks of Cypress Creek. I still have seven of my children; in all I reared a dozen to maturity. Since then I have lost three daughters; the oldest, Dora, in the year 1919, Johanna in the year 1927, and our poor Paula in the year 1924. But as long as I lived in the new home, called "Cherry Home," I still had the twelve children: six sons and six daughters.

From about 1889 we also had our niece Cora Fuchs with us, who since her mother had died had lived with Brother-in-law Conrad's family. In 1893, she went to San Antonio to attend school. Her father married again soon. Then we often had lively, merry times, for Cora Fuchs was a very lively child. Dina and the three youngest also understood how to banish silence. Besides this we also associated actively with our relatives, the Goeths and the Fritz Fuchses (Fritz Fuchs is a half-cousin of your grandfather Fuchs). Both families lived near us. Distant friends and relatives also visited us and we visited them. Many happy feasts were celebrated, and many people came to attend them, among others the Struves, Richters, Schroeters, Gieseckes, Kellersbergers, Ebelings, Materns, Goebels, and many more, in spite of the fact that the horses feet could not take the people about as quickly as the cars can today.

The young people danced in the house, and played many different kinds of games outdoors. Later a Rifle Club Hall was built for the inhabitants of Cypress Creek, and it was near our house, which as a result of course brought us even more visitors. At Shovel Mountain the Rifle Club Society had long had a hall; now the two societies often invited each other and held very nice celebrations under different presidents, [August] Schroeter and [Julius] Kellersberger, for example. Both did much to create entertainment. Also, the old teacher F. G. Schaupp delivered many nice lectures, read poems, as well as rendered other beautiful programs.

Each society owned a piano, and on them accompaniments for songs were played, and in the evening Fritz Reiner and Ernst Goeth played four-handed pieces for dances. Two pieces, "The Rifle Club Waltz" and "The Shepherd Waltz," which Fritz Reiner had composed, were especially favorite dances with the young people. They also met with approval in Germany, where he sent them. They were not printed, for he only copied them by hand.

In the year 1885 my oldest daughter Dora married Fritz Reiner, but after five or six years she became a widow, and her three small children grew up to be capable adults without having known their father. Each of the children had musical talent. Marie, the oldest, is now Mrs. Franz Herbst of Gause, Texas. She has a son and daughter. The second, Sophia, Mrs. Hyatt, is also the mother of two children, a daughter and a son; Hermann, who lives on his parents' place, very close to our "Cherry Home," with his wife, born Esther Wedekind, a former teacher, has one son.

But I am hurrying forward too rapidly!

After Fritz Reiner died, Dora moved to us with her three children. The teacher Heyer moved with his wife and child into Dora's house and taught in a new Rifle Club Hall that had been built on a hill on our land. — On its opening night Fritz Reiner had played for a dance for the last time. — He had given our children lessons in music and as a private teacher had also given them instructions in other subjects. On the day of his death, Louise at his wish played *Weber's Last Thought* for him on the piano. That was in April, 1890.

Here I should like to mention that Reiner taught our children duets, and in the Goeths' house at Grandfather Fuchs' coffin they sang *In the Grave Is Rest* in duet form; that was in December, 1885.

Unfortunately, Father Fuchs had to suffer for several months before his death, and your papa rode over every evening and helped nurse him, and he always looked forward with pleasure to Papa's coming. Grandfather's last words were, "Behold the path with roses!"

The year before that Grandfather and Grandmother Fuchs had both been with us for several weeks, during a period when Ottilie Goeth (Tilie) could not be at home and take care of her parents because her own daughter needed her. They liked to stay with us, and we enjoyed having them. I am still thankful today that I always got along so well with my parents-in-law; I felt that they liked me, and that still makes me happy today. And all the difficulties of the past years were therefore much easier to bear. The following comes from an obituary by Fritz Reiner for Grandfather Fuchs:

> *Everlasting peace be with your soul!*
> *Thou now has parted from us.*
>
> *You have emptied the cup of sorrows;*
> *Fought the last battle!*
> *Now you are redeemed from your sorrow –*
> *Rejoice, Father, in your salvation!*
>
> *But your image shall always,*
> *As long as we stay on this earth,*
> *Stand before our souls!*
> *And if our hearts are as noble as yours,*
> *We are hopeful for a blessed meeting!*

In March, 1886, Grandmother Fuchs died. She never recovered from Grandfather's death, but she still took pleasure in her youngest grandchild, Johanna, Hermann and Lina's youngest. "She has a small, round apple face!"; those were her words. Otti Goeth and Ulli Matern, her granddaughters, now Mrs. Otto Wenmohs and Mrs. Walter Giesecke, faithfully helped nurse her. Here I will follow with one of the many poems that Grandfather wrote for his "Mudding."

To My Dear Wife for Her Forty-Third Birthday

(written in the year 1852, the last year we lived in Cat Spring)

> *Yes, to be sure you are today forty-three!*
> *But your lips still slow so fresh and spicy;*
> *And if in dancing you no longer quickly*
>   *twirl,*
> *Your eyes are bright as the lightning's flash!*

And if you are at times a little peevish,
Soon you are gracious and kissable
again.
Therefore remain but tranquil, be quiet
and serene:
Then our wedded stream will flow
gaily on!

My own good mother had died three years before Grandmother Fuchs, on March 8, 1883. Unfortunately, neither Lina nor I could go there to help nurse her. She also had to suffer for a while. Our good sister Ida faithfully nursed her, as she later lovingly cared for our lonely father, in which she was assisted by Brother Johannes and his wife, who lived on our parents' place.

At her coffin Johannes' wife spoke the words of Paul Heyse's:

Into the earth we lower your body,
Yet always we will lovingly think of
you;
In your image all the strength and
kindness,
Shall give us comfort.
You lived a pure life here below,
Surrounded by love, life's gift to you.
Sleep! We others will wander on,
Through battle to peace!

After that Werner Perlitz spoke the words:
"*Hard towards herself, but always with loving consideration for others even to her last hour; endeavoring to do right so far as she understood it — that was the chief attribute of dear Grandmother Romberg. May this also be said of us when we die.*"

In the Spring 1884

A poem by Grandfather Johannes Romberg

The time for spring has come again,
The fount of life flows and leaps,
And everything is greening fair,
The flowers bloom, the sparrows sing.

A breath of sadness seems to hover
On all this earthly splendor;
For she no longer breathes and lives
Who made life dear to me.

A dreadful silence reigns
Around the cold deceased,
If I draw near to plead and listen,
The grave remains tyrannically mute!

Above the ground Spring calls for life!
The woods drive forth the budding green.
Below me in the cold, dark earth
A human body falls to dust.

I do not know if the soul will live
And if there be some future meeting,
No human heart but falters
On thought of death as dreadful victor.

To be or not to be — yet who can say?
We stand enfolded by some mighty Power.
Be silenced then, you vain complaints,
This greater Power has ordered life: go let it
  be.

But now the spring has come again.
Your hearts respond to all its beauties!
The little singers tune their songs,
And frolic in the azure sky.

The earth is beautiful and so is life,
And youth is like the springtime,
Where life's germ sprouts and strives,
Where everything's abloom both near and
    far.

Silenced today be every complaint,
I warm myself in the sunshine,
And when my days have passed away,
Lower me to rest beside her grave.

If then another day may dawn or no,
Rosy and fair in a lovelier land?
We lie there sheltered and softly hid
Held up in the arms of our Mother Earth.

You children, who remain awhile
On this resplendent star,
May you dearly love each other all
And kindly help each other all you can.

But I, still living, gladly greet
The sunshine's golden stream —
And when it glooms — you also, Stars,
Countless in the wide sky's dome.

I greet you too, you old gray Earth
Whose child I am. You nourished me,
And when I'm turned to lifeless dust,
I shall slumber in my mother's arms.

In the Spring 1886

Storms blow about the house
And whistle o'er the shaking roof,
But then they come no more with icy breath
From far-flung snowfields of the North,
They are the heralds sent by Spring
To shake the towering forest trees

And rouse them rudely from their winter's
   trance.

And now, to the breezes' gentle song,
A stir of life begins,
Coaxed awake by the warming rays
Of the kindly springtime sun.

All the buds are swelling;
E'en in the earth's deep lap
The bursting seeds are rising to the light,
Bursting through the clod,
And violet's blossoms too
Are opening between the leaves,
A green protecting roof;
Fragrance wafts from all the lovely flowers.
And then those bitter days
Come back to memory,
Those days my wife grew sick
And felt Death nearing her.
We brought her then
A blossoming violet to her room.
She breathed the fragrance of
That messenger of spring,
But Spring itself,
She did not live to see.
Long she rested in the lap
Of the hallowed earth.

'Tis true, the wound is healing now
That ached so sharply then,
But grieving memory stays,
And no day passes by
Without regretful thought of her.
Life has become so desolate,
And out of past and darkness,
Out of the days far gone,
I strive to recall and bring to light
The many happy days and years,
The sunny springtime of our love.

Almost half a hundred years
We lived together, happy.
When we had scarce outgrown our
  childhood,
Our hearts in love united.
"Part!" That word was
Cruelly spoken by Fate.
And now I stand alone. Alone?
Heart, do not be ungrateful.

Happy have I lived,
Great joy was mine on earth,
And even in these days of grief
My loved ones are about me.
What e'er afflicted me in life
Shall be forgotten; now may rest
In the twilight of the past. I will
Rejoice among my loved ones;
I'll greet with happy heart
In the spring the birds'
Singing and the flowers,
And spring's awakening growth.

Twice your Grandparents Romberg visited in the mountains together, during the time when we lived by the mill. As long as she was there, Mother taught you older children as well as Lina's foster children, Walter and Marietta Anderson, at our house and Sister Lina's. Father often stayed with us, and then the fathers Fuchs and Romberg always entertained each other very well— very frequently in Mecklenburger "platt," especially when they were teasing each other or indulging in satire on political subjects.

He was also present when we still lived on the "Oasis" after the war and had a large Fourth of July celebration. All the relatives and friends in the neighborhood were there. They had ordered a barrel of beer from

Pressler in Austin, speeches were held, and everyone was in a good humor because at last there was peace again. One of the tables which we had made by splitting a large poplar tree that was "sacrificed" for the occasion, is still in use on the butchering days at our place,"Cherry Home" (which is now Adolf's home). The two halves of the tree served at that particular Fourth of July celebration as banquet table, with boards that were placed from one to the other. The large, long half of the tree trunk was on each end of the half-round side fastened to legs. — It is possible that there are similar tables in parks today.

But where have I wandered to again? I wanted to tell of our life at "Cherry Home."

When Reiner was no longer living, Moritz and John Goebel, with their violins, joined Ernst Goeth to furnish music for the dances. Later Eddie, Tilie and Carl Goeth's third son, was a very popular piano player at dances. Moritz and John Goebel also often played with him. But the young people did not only dance. Now and then there were school programs and other entertainments, in which the young people of the neighborhood participated. Sometimes, summer guests, relatives, and friends from the cities also did their part. Little operettas were sometimes performed. Once they were so ambitious as to perform "Bohemian Girl," abridged of course. It required much preparation but also furnished much pleasure. I can also say that of the little operettas that Daughter Louise practiced with the school children at different times.

Louise, who had not married, as four of my other daughters did (and three of them as early as eighteen years) wished to improve herself in music. As money was no longer so scarce, Papa fulfilled her wish. He himself was also very fond of music. Of course there were still many improvements to be wished for in the house, but, on the other hand, I later enjoyed many nice songs sung by Louise, and she afterwards could teach many nieces and nephews music, as well as other children in the neighborhood or in other places, where she was a music teacher for many years; and she could help in school concerts, and at "Sängerfests." In all respects it has made her life much richer.

She especially enjoyed a stay in Germany, where she received vocal instruction (in Berlin), as well as heard wonderful music. Also the excursions along the Rhine and in Switzerland which she made in the company of her niece, Bertha Hoppe (now the widow of Walter Richter). She said that it was so wonderful there, and she had to think of her Grandfather Fuchs (whose singing she remembered so well, also that he let her sing, and sang with her) and of this song, words as well as music of his composition: "When the Singer Travels through the Wild Forest!" And she sang it, until it echoed among the rocks:

> *When the singer walks through the wild*
> * forest,*
> *And his song sounds through flowers,*
> * foliage, and trees,*
> *Now like soft wind and then with stormlike*
> * force,*
> *Then everything that lives there gives ear,*
> *Even the flower's soft eyes look up at him,*
> *And the birds all join in the chorus.*
> *Everything, everything enjoys his songs,*
> *E'en the cold rocks resound them again.*
>
> *When the singer's song is brought to the*
> * people's ear,*
> *When it sounds in palaces and in the huts,*
> *When it sings of love and joy, and battles*
> * and freedom,*
> *Ha, how many a heart is then uplifted,*

Ha, how many then do beat in joy and pain,
And many a bright eye then sinks
    downward,
For the singer awakens deep yearning
And tears take the place of joy.

Hail! O hail the singer who thus succeeds,
Who kindles the sacred fire in human
    hearts,
When it sings of love and joy, and war and
    freedom.
Singing is beautiful in a lonesome forest,
Where the songs resound through flowers,
    leaves and branches,
But thrice more beautiful, when it echoes,
Through the chambers of congenial hearts,
Alike in joy and alike in pain.

During this stay in Germany Louise visited relatives in Doberan, Rostock, Schwerin, and Berlin. She is still in correspondence with one aunt, and also, together with Frieda Fuchs, supported a former teacher, Amalie Gensler, during and after the War.

For several summers, in our home and in Brother-in-law Hermann's, we enjoyed beautiful music, as Brother Johannes' son Walter and Brother-in-law Bennie's son Oscar, who had come back from Switzerland and from Leipzig, where they had studied music, were spending their vacations with us. They generously rendered wonderful music, and the musical relatives here came and added their best efforts also. One summer Oscar had a choir consisting of the young girls about Cypress. Hedwig Romberg (Brother Johannes' daughter), was also with us that summer and participated, as well as Johanna Fuchs (Hermann and Lina's daughter), who came the long road over the rocks from "Colorado Valley View Home," as Hermann called his place to our "Cherry

Home" or to the Kellersbergers at the mill. (Julius Kellersberger had bought the mill from us.)

Most of this was rehearsal, while the result was later presented free of charge in the hall. Oscar Fox often spoke of the pleasure that this choir gave him because of the good voices and the musical execution that he was able to develop in that short time: Certainly a fine inheritance from Grandfather Fuchs and other musical ancestors!

Here I shall also mention that many a nice wedding eve was celebrated in the hall, for which suitable passages for recitation were found in books, though often changes were made in the text to fit the particular occasion. Or something original was written in prose or doggerel, as well as other kinds of verse, to honor the young couple, in jest and earnest, by relatives or friends, who either were appointed to do it or felt a call to write. And it was always something pleasant and charming to which the young couple listened, sitting on a decorated throne, surrounded by foliage and flowers. A "Kaffeeklatsch," or a gypsy procession, the latter decorated in brightest colors and held with song and music, dances around the campfire, as well as fortune-telling, particularly aroused gaiety and interest.

There were also many picnics for old and young, beside a spring or near a nice mountain view or on the Pedernales or the Colorado, at Easter, the Fourth of July, or on birthdays, etc. These were popular and attracted happy guests. Or there were excursions to the mountains, for example, to the little or the big Castle Mountain near the Colorado, named so by Grandfather Fuchs; to the Granite Mountain on the north side of the Colorado River, where many rocks were quarried and shipped to construct large buildings, for example, the Texas Capitol, and the sea-wall at Galveston, etc.

Excursions were also made to Indian caves, to stalactite caves at Hamilton Pool, and other interesting places. How the picnic lunch was relished or the meal after the return home: Lina and Elsie Perlitz often went along on such excursions, as well as Anna (Annie) Romberg, children of my youngest sister and brother, who at different times were teachers here at Cypress, at Marble Falls, and at Shovel Mountain.

In the year 1886 we celebrated our silver wedding day, a nice celebration with many relatives and friends present. The teacher F. G. Schaupp wrote us a poem, which still hangs framed in my room. Our married life was a happy one, in spite of many difficulties which we had to bear together, and although later, when the different children expressed their wish to learn this or that, sometimes differences of opinion appeared. I wanted to fulfill their wishes, as much as possible, while Papa was of the opinion that much schooling and going out into the world did not make people happier or better,. Yet he provided the younger sons with a private teacher. Old Mr. George Stolley lived with us for years and taught especially Reinhold and Adolf. In spite of much work, school hours were conscientiously observed as much as possible.

The wish of our youngest, Johannes, called Hans, to become an attorney, was fulfilled. He probably also had received the best preschooling at home, since in later years we had better teachers than at first. He received his first instruction at the age of three from my niece Lina Perlitz. Hans, at the time of our silver wedding a baby of half a year, was always the most affectionate of all my children. Whether it was really his nature, or whether it was because I was no longer so overwhelmed with work as in the first years, I cannot judge.

Perhaps he had the nature of my father, who was always more tenderly affectionate than my mother. As long as I can remember, Father always had a "Good-morning kiss" for Mother, and in the evening before supper, in the twilight, while one child attended to the milking and another placed supper on the table, they walked up and down in front of the house, arm in arm, and talked.

Brother Johannes and his wife also had this custom. Good Sister Ida was there and attended to half the work, so that they had more time for each other. Here I think of Sister Lina's youngest, Johanna, also named after Father; she also was always an affectionate little thing. How many loving kisses she had for Father and Mother! The youngest is frequently noticed more by others in the family, and more time is devoted to him, as was the case with us. It may have been an advantage for Hans.

In justice to Reinhold's talents, he should also have had more schooling. How often he entertained his brothers and sisters with funny, extemporaneous lectures! But even then he also showed a great predilection for horses. As a small boy he enjoyed playing with a little tin horse. Later he would dearly have liked to be a cowboy. Adolf wished to study more; but he had great success as a farmer and goat breeder.

Hans later attended the University [of Texas in Austin] after he had received good private instruction. As a small boy he generally preferred to stay at home, reading or playing with his nephew Hermann Reiner. Daughter Louise later with an "absolute command" managed to get him to go along to a celebration, with the remonstrances: "It is better for you to go, or it will always be harder for you to force yourself to go." He often made speeches to his young nephews, to which they listened with interest.

Once while Hans was plowing in a field situated on a hill, he saw that the Pedernales was quickly rising. His two nephews were fishing below the Falls, and he knew that they were in danger. He ran to warn them as fast as he could, one mile, and reached them just in time before the high water came over the Falls.

Daughter Ida married John Goebel on October 8, 1887, the year after our silver wedding; as a girl she was always cheerful, and as a woman she kept her gay temperament. She lives on the same place on Cypress Creek, where George and Hanni first had their home. Her oldest son, Moritz, is manager of the large printing office of Baylor University in Waco. He was first married to Agnes Dietz, and now to her sister Hester. His first wife died after a few years and left two children; the second wife presented him with two more.

This Moritz Goebel is my oldest grandchild, and his daughter Lucille, my oldest great-grandchild. He especially asked my to write down my reminiscences. At this time I want to take occasion to mention each of the families of my children, for I have learned how quickly relatives can lose track of their relationships to each other. And it might be a good idea if you would preserve this as a family tree. If this book has given you pleasure, you must thank my oldest grandson, who set the stone to rolling.

The second son, Berthold, was very musically gifted. He also worked himself up in his vocation, but he had to give up his profession as a music teacher when he was drafted as a soldier in the year 1917. Soon a fatal attack of pneumonia brought to an end his very uncongenial soldier's life. He is one of the many, many war victims.

The sisters Laura and Louise Goebel make their home in Lockhart, Texas, the wives of Oscar Seeliger and Carl Schubert, merchants. The first has two dear little girls, and the latter has a son and daughter. Willie Goebel, the next, is married to Irmgard Lechow. They have two sons and live on the parents' farm. Norma, the third daughter, also has a nice talent for music. She is married to Victor Wenmohs; they have one little daughter, Bernice. Anton, the fourth son, plays the violin in masterly style, with deep feeling. In July, 1927, he took Grace Christ for his life companion. Ludwig, the youngest son, is a teacher, and he, as well as Anton, graduated from Baylor University. Ludwig also has musical talent. Both earned their way through school. Gladys, still a child in school, likewise shows musical talent.

Theodor, our oldest son, lives a distance north of here in a new, nicely arranged home with his wife Helene, foster-daughter of Joseph Giger and his wife, born Auguste Varnhagen. Auguste is intellectually very active and well-read and also has the ability to relate what she has read in an interesting way. And if someone is in need of nursing, she is a first-rate nurse. Here I also think of daughter Dora, who so often helped out in time of sickness wherever it was necessary.

The farm of Theodor and Helene, and that of their sons, Hugo and Hellmuth, border upon each other. The two latter were both drafted in the military service in 1915; Hugo for a short time before the Armistice was quartermaster in France. He was once very sick and has a war comrade to thank for his life. Hellmuth lived a short time in Austin, where he faithfully nursed a friend. Gertrude Hyatt was at that time already Hugo's bride. She then became his wife, and now they are the parents of three sons and one daughter. Hellmuth married a teacher, Mary Redford; unfortunately they lost their little son. The third son, Joseph, a chemical engineer employed by the Portland Cement Company, was in the Argentine two years, where his bride, Ruby Riley of Fredericksburg, followed him, when she had finished her studies. Theodor's only daughter, Leonora, is married to a farmer, Lloyd Lester, and is the mother of three daughters and one son. Conrad, the youngest son, has a position as a cotton classifier.

My son Willie was always very industrious and practical; already as a young man he was very systematic. He lives to the west of us with his wife, Selma Goeth (daughter of the musician Ernst Goeth); she is thorough in her house-keeping, and of her one can say: she is always ready.

Lydia, Willie's only daughter, was for a long time occupied as a bookkeeper in San Antonio. Later she graduated as a nurse and became superintendent of the Kleberg County Hospital in Kingsville. The oldest son, Alex, died in his sixteenth year. Bernhard, now the only one at home, is a goat-breeder and a mechanic on the farm and for his neighbors. The third son, Lothar, was always sickly. Romberg, the youngest, is a student in the San Antonio Technical School.

Daughter Dina married earlier than Willie, in January of the same year [1894]; Clemens Ebeling is her life companion. Of both these couples it can be said that opposites attract. In both cases the women are livelier than the men, even if both couples are very different in other respects.

Dina, like my sister Lina, always took pleasure in teasing, and also liked to do nice hand-work and was skillful at it. She kept her cheerfulness in spite of ill health and much that was hard in her life. She, also, had to give up one of her children, her little Adalbert, who was a sweet, friendly little boy. He and her youngest daughter, Otelia, were born in Plainview in Hale County. The four oldest children were born in Marble Falls, where Clemens had a shop. They have traveled much with Otelia the last years, frequently staying a long time with us. Last winter they were with their daughter Amanda in Lockhart. Now for health's sake they are in New Mexico, for Clemens suffers with asthma, and Dina with diabetes.

Their oldest son, Ernst, lives on their well-improved farm, six miles from Plainview. He married a nurse, Harriet Marquardt, a friend of his sister Amanda, who studied with her in Temple. They have a little family of four consisting of twins, a girl and a boy, and two other children.

Leo, the second son, was with his cousin Adolf Hoppe in Pennsylvania as an engineer, where he met a girl named Helen Osborne and brought her to Texas as his bride. They were very sad to have to lose their firstborn child.

Julius, the youngest son, chose Else Ebeling for his life companion, a daughter of Max and Toni Ebeling and great-grandchild of old Adolf Wenmohs. They have a little son, and their home is in Kress, Texas, where Julius is manager of a lumber company.

Amanda, the oldest child, married last. Walter Bodemann is her husband, and they have a nice home on their farm near Lockhart, Texas. In July of this year a little daughter was born to them, my youngest great-grandchild, whom they soon want to show to its great-grandmother.

When Amanda visited here for the first time with her husband, we related many stories, also some about my brothers and sisters, and it was mentioned that my youngest sister first saw the light of this world on a stormy sea. Then Amanda's husband asked, "Was her life also a stormy one?" We answered, "At all events it was not a quiet, easy life!"

My youngest sister, Rike, was left a widow with seven daughters and one son, who was not yet of school age. On the farm and later in the city, they all studied and worked with all their strength, in order to make a living. The oldest daughter and her husband died and left behind three little girls, who were brought up by the grandmother and aunts. Some of Rike's daughters are teachers and graduates of the University and have accomplished something.

The oldest of the Eberle girls, the three little grandchildren, became a teacher, the second a sculptor in Chicago, and the youngest a journalist. This youngest girl, like the oldest, exercises her profession in New York. The names of the girls are Hulda, Elisabeth, and Irmgard Eberle.

This spring Sister Rike Perlitz was with me and related many things about her life and her trip to Chicago, Buffalo, and New York in the year 1926 to visit several of her grandchildren and children.

Her daughter Lina, who before her marriage to Helon MacFarland, was many years a teacher and Dean of the College of Industrial Arts in Denton, Texas, sent her the money for the trip, so that she could show her mother her home in Buffalo, after enjoying herself in the large cities. It was a pleasure for me to hear about all the relatives, especially of Marie, her second daughter, who as a girl and young woman painted a great deal, and later also drew wild flowers for her husband Bernhard Mackensen's botanical writings or reports for school and scientific societies, and who now, after she has been a widow for years, and her three children are independent, is again taking lessons in art at C.I.A. in Denton. Everything Rike told interested me, also how she always had cheerful jokes interspersed with many earnest thoughts.

At Easter I had another pleasure: Brother Bernhard's youngest son, Arnold Romberg, with his wife and Rike's daughter, Elsie, came from Austin to take Sister Rike home. What a pleasure it must be for Brother Bernhard that his son could study the same subject that always interested him, so that he now is Professor of Physics at the State University. And that Elsie Perlitz teaches German there also makes Sister Rike and me happy. Now

Rike is at home again and takes care of the members of her household and her flowers—always cheerful and brave. In that we are similar; both have to see something blooming and in spite of much work must take care of a few flowers.

Papa also took pleasure in flowers and the beauties of nature. Almost always when he had been away, he brought me back something—wild flowers, or peculiar rocks, or other things.

When he went off, he always liked to take me along in the spring to sell wool thirty to fifty miles away, to Burnet and Austin, which I enjoyed doing in later years when the children were old enough to take over the work at home.

In the year 1889 he took me and two daughters to Austin to the State "Sängerfest," and ten years later, 1899, he took me to Beeville, where Daughter Louise taught at that time and helped direct a concert. The year before we had gone in a hack with our youngest to my old home, to the silver wedding of my uncle Hermann Bauch. The celebration was very festive, with much entertainment.

A few years before, we three had also visited my father and shown him his youngest grandchild and namesake. While we were there, Hans said, "I will sit on this little 'Tlitt'," by which he meant a small footstool. When we drove through a rough place in the Pedernales on our return home, he said, "Here I will build a bridge someday, when I am big!" A bridge stands there now, but he did not build it.

We made an interesting trip by hack to San Antonio. (This old hack was borrowed by many a bridegroom to get his life companion with). We visited Sister Rike and other relatives there. On our return we stayed in New Braunfels with a Hoffmann family while it rained and learned that their parents had come over on the same ship with the Fuchses.

Once when Papa was in Austin, he met Brother-in-law Conrad's son Adolf (Adolph C.), who tuned pianos there, and suggested to him that he start a quarry at Lueders, as he had the mechanical knowledge. His father had also once owned a steam mill at Tiger Creek. Adolf agreed to this, and Papa bought the machinery for it. This land at Lueders belonged to the estate of Grandfather Fuchs; it had been given to him by his friend [Mayor Carl Friedrich Wilhelm Lueders of Marlow, Germany, whose brother Ferdinand] Lueders had fought in the Mexican War [Texas War of Independence against Mexico in1836] and had received the land as payment. He had no use for it, as he was returning to Germany, and gave it to Grandfather Fuchs, who wanted to emigrate to Texas. Son Julius and Adolf Fox worked there together, and later our son Adolf was also with them there for a short time. Your papa had the pleasure of seeing them make a success of it.

On the ranch on the Pedernales we had cattle and horses and a large flock of sheep, for which we had to have shepherds in the early years. When the sheep had been sold and the debts paid, Papa bought one thousand goats, which at that time still had to be herded. Now they all run free in small pastures.

After the sons were grown and could take care of the field and cattle, Papa was elected County Commissioner; for six years he faithfully went out to perform the duties of his office.

He was a zealous member of the Freemasons and rode regularly to lodge meetings, a distance of fifteen miles, until a short time before his death. On August 20, 1903, he suddenly died of heart failure in his sixty-fifth year, after he had mowed the weeds in the orchard and come into the house with fruit in his hands.

It was a hard blow for us, and yet we were glad that he did not have to suffer long, for he had often complained and was very excitable.

He had a better death than his brothers Conrad and Bennie, who had died before him, and his younger brother Hermann, who outlived him several years, as well as his sister Ulla Matern Varnhagen, who lived to be over eighty years old, and Ottilie Goeth, who was a little over ninety years old. Both were widows many years. Aunt Ulla was faithfully nursed by her daughter Lulu Ebeling, and Aunt Tilie spent her last years with her daughter Otti Wenmohs, of whom she always said, "My Ottichen nurses me as a mother her child!"

Now I am the last remaining of the old generation. Uncle Fritz Fuchs and Aunt Theodora for years have lived on the plains in north Texas, as well as their grown children with their families.

Soon after Papa's death Adolf came back from Lueders and took over the place, as Reinhold preferred to work with cattle. When the land in Lueders was sold, Hans was able to attend the University; our house was more conveniently arranged, and I allowed myself a visit to my brothers and sisters. First to San Antonio to Sister Rike; from there to Flatonia to visit Adolf and Anna Wenmohs, who were always dear friends of mine; then to my brother Johannes and his family in Schulenburg. With them I visited Brother Bernhard and his wife Lina, who is no longer living; only Bernhard still lives near our old home, with his son Ernst.

At my wish Bernhard took me to the graves of our parents. As my father had always said, "Do not set a stone above my head!", it was difficult to find the graves.

Aunt Ida traveled on with me to Gonzales, where I saw my niece, Marie Fouts, born Franke, as well as Hans Romberg, a lawyer, Bernhard's oldest son.

My niece Cora, married to Heinrich [Henry Clay] von Struve, at that time lived there. Later they lived in different lands, where he officiated as a consul. We had already known the family Struve in Fayette County and in later years were good friends of theirs.

In El Campo we visited our oldest sister, Bernhardine, and her sons, Heinrich, Paul, Bennie, and Hermann, owners of large rice fields. They showed us their irrigation systems.

The trip and the meeting with all my loved ones was a pleasure to me; I also saw some friends of my youth, Anna Kloss-Willerich, Hermine Richers-Nordhausen, Mr. and Mrs. Engel, and others. When in September, 1927, I was looking for a poem by my dear Sister-in-law Berline, by a strange coincidence I received it at the same time from my dear friend, Donate Pellar. Her father, Adolf Wenmohs, had once copied it, and she had obtained it through her sister Alexe of Flatonia. I will copy this beautiful poem for you:

My Summer

In the old house, so plain and gray,
The old farmer and I, the wife.
Free through the hall the south wind blows,
The corn is ripening in the field.
The cotton fields are white as snow,
The sun above so hot! so hot!
Oh somber life, how beautiful you are!

The daughter sweet, bride of my son,
The daughter-in-law so loving and dear,
And grandchildren too, how splendid they
  are!
Out of eyes so clear the future laughs.
We are sitting outside, our little flock,
The stars above, so wonderful!
What one thinks in silence,

Some other speaks in words.

They hold debates and share disputes
But still they never grudge and quarrel,
They all see truth and knowledge,
In all the father's spirit flames.
Yet error sometimes enters in,
And also folly, to our shame!
And sorrows come, they never fail
To accompany our melody.

And there is work from morn till late.
A quiet joy my evening prayer,
No other time for meditation,
The will is always primed for action.
Yet heart and head are warm and clear.
So may it be for many a year,
We both wish that, I know it well,
The ageing farmer and his wife.

Now back to my children. Adolf, the second youngest son, was of a quiet nature as a child, but later he was often rather reckless and enterprising. He started going to parties and dances very early, and he was a skillful dancer. He still is, though now father of three sons and three daughters.

In 1910 he married Georgia Bell Wilkerson. She was a teacher for four years, and perhaps that is why she is such a good hand at bringing up children. Adolf also has talent for that. Because for a while we lived near each other, the three oldest children, Thomas, Elmyre, and Adalbert (Albert), at first learned the German language, although the mother spoke only English. The three youngest, A.D., Jr. (Adolf), Opal Louise, and Lucy May, speak only English. So also do Reinhold's children, for he likewise has an American of English descent for a wife, Martina, born Henslee. They married in the year 1918. She is a clever, skillful woman and knows very well how to dress herself and the children tastefully. Henslee, Lillian, and Madeline are her three girls.

Johannes graduated from the University in the year 1909, and possibly because he spoke the German language, he at once found occupation as an attorney in New Braunfels. He still lives there with his wife and two sons.

His school comrade and early friend, Patty Wenmohs, daughter of John and Louise Wenmohs, became his wife in the year 1911. As his wife she is still his good comrade, with a lively and active mind.

The oldest son, Markus, is already attending high school. He told me this summer that he wants to be either a lawyer or a journalist.

John, Jr., his brother, is full of life. These two grandchildren have already made interesting trips with their parents, something for which I have always longed, though it was only lately that I have had a chance. I have several times been in San Antonio, and once I visited a large Exposition. In the evening there was a performance of The Ruin of Pompeii. By day already you could see the smoke rising out of a large mountain; in the evening the Olympic Games were held, and after that the catastrophe occurred, with thunder, smoke and fire. This was all outdoors. I once saw Faust, and heard the singer Madam Schumann-Heink sing. In Fredericksburg I heard the Wiener Truppe and also saw a beautiful slide show, "The Rhine," there.

In the year 1913 I made a journey with Julius, visiting my grandson Moritz Goebel in Waco and my daughter Dina Ebeling and family in Plainview, as well as my many other relatives and friends, Fuchses and Struves. In 1904 Julius came back from the quarry because the work and the life there did not please him. He likes to read scientific things; romances do not interest him. He

Our Home Near The Pedernales

is a zealous Freemason. He likes to play with his nephews and nieces and other children, and they all like him.

In the year 1916 we left our "Cherry Home" and moved with Julius to his piece of land. (I had divided the property among all my children.) We thought it best to leave Adolf alone with his family, hard as it was to leave the old place and the children, of whom I was so fond and whom I had helped take care of ever since they were small and who also thought much of their grandmother. Now I have for many years had the pleasure of seeing them pass by at school-time every morning with their gay, friendly "Good mornings." And in the afternoon they bring the mail, letters from Dina and Hans, the only children in the distance, and from other dear ones, as well as the German newspaper Das Wochenblatt from Austin, published by Mr. Trenckmann, which we have read for years. At first it was Texas Vorwärts, edited by Julius Schuetze.

Our move was in various respects advantageous: Julius had a home of his own now. Louise could give piano lessons, since the school was near; the schoolchildren came and learned to sing songs to piano accompaniment.

For many years a new school has stood near our store and post office. Two teachers have frequently been employed there. One year we had as teacher Ino Varnhagen, grandchild of my early friend and sister-in-law, Ino Fuchs Varnhagen, and later her sister Dora was teacher in our school for three years. Both were excellent teachers. Still another gifted teacher whom I would like to mention was Professor Heinrich Sibberns, who came to Texas through his friend Theodor Saul, a relative of the Rombergs.' Our Hans, as well as many other young men, received training preparatory to going to the University and other schools from Professor Sibberns. He especially understood how to awaken the desire for more knowledge, particularly interest in things worth knowing.

He lodged in the home of my sister-in-law Ottilie Goeth and her daughter Louise Wenmohs' home during his work here as a teacher. He was a real friend to Sister Ottilie when he assisted her to write down her reminiscences, Was Grossmutter Erzählt (Memoirs of a Texas Pioneer Grandmother).

When Louise Wenmohs was with us recently and we spoke of Lindbergh's great deed, his daring to fly alone over the ocean and his success, she said, "The daily sacrifice of a real teacher in faithful work is rarely paid as highly as it deserves and is in truth worth more than the performance of Charles Lindbergh."

I remember that it used to be said, "Men will never fly; for that is impossible." And yet I have lived to see airships fly by near us over valleys and mountains. What all you grandchildren and great-grandchildren may not live to see and help accomplish! You must never think that there is nothing more to investigate and to improve.

Unfortunately, the well on Julius' place does not give enough water, so I could not have as many flowers as on the old place. Julius drilled for water several hundred feet deep, but to no purpose. He only had great expenses.

The World War years, as well as the following ones, were hard years. In four years I lost three daughters, and Daughter Louise's health was not good. Otherwise, I could probably have started much sooner on my "Reminiscences," and it would not have been so hard for me.

In the last few years we frequently had Daughter Dina, her husband, and daughter Otelia with us for long visits, also her oldest daughter Amanda, who said to me, "Grandmother, at your house it is always so cozy.

Other grandchildren also came visiting from distant places, as well as dear friends. My son Hans and family always spend the Christmas holidays in the old house, and in the summer they camp and fish.

Daughter Dina always enjoys walking on the hill near our house, and when two years ago we drove with her to Horseshoe Bend, she was so enthusiastic and could not understand why as a young girl she had never been there. She said, "That is as beautiful and romantic as Denver, Colorado!"

Yes, unfortunately, the beauties of nature are not admired enough; children's attention should be called to them more.

When I was in New Braunfels to visit Hans and his family, I again and again admired the beautiful Comal Springs.

Three years ago when we visited Sister Lina and her daughter Frieda (they live near their daughter and sister Johanna, who is married to Alfred Schnelle, son of Carl and Emma Schnelle), we made an excursion, of which my niece Frieda Fuchs wrote the following:

"It was a Sunday, bright and clear, one of the rarest days in the year.' So I thought on August 17, 1924, although bright, sunny days have not, for a long time, belonged to the rarities, and although still other songs were in my mind, like *Am Rhein, Für Musik, and Ach, wer das doch könnte, nur ein einziges, ein einziges Mal!,* as they had sounded throughout our rooms before we made an excursion with dear relatives to the 'Balancing Rock' near Fredericksburg.

"Fly, yes, if one could do that! But we were content that three cars could hold twenty-one people, and we started happily on our way, as the clear bright day bowed to the approaching night. Our supper, which should refresh us after our climb of the mountain, also was stored in the cars. How pleasant was the long shadow of the hill rising to the west near Bear Mountain. We had expected our mothers would prefer to rest in the shade while younger, even if no longer so very young, feet would climb to the heights. But my mother, as the youngest of three sisters, took hurried steps to the foot of the hill, and the sisters, eighty-four and eighty-one years old, followed her energetically. When we younger ones perceived our mothers' determination to climb to the top, Frank Stanford helped the eighty-four-year-old Aunt Louise Fuchs, and I went to my seventy-eight-year-old mother's side. But our Aunt Ida Romberg asserted: 'I can go best and surest alone.' Characteristic of her, for all her life she was without a companion, although she was never 'alone,' for she was the favorite of her brothers and sisters, nieces and nephews, and to the latter she was always a motherly friend.

"The ascent of and the visit on the 'Balancing Rock' probably also had a special attraction for the sisters because their brother, in spite of his eighty-two years, had lately climbed the mountain. His lively narrative of the natural phenomena of the mountain had probably lured them to want to see it for themselves. For Uncle Bernhard Romberg the visit was particularly interesting, as he had an active interest in human beings, in their physical character and their welfare (natural science, physics).

"Bernhard Romberg said, 'That I have seen Fredericksburg and its vicinity is very interesting to me.' And now we were standing where he had also stood several weeks before, wondering and marveling how that miracle had happened, the large round stone standing so secure and solid on its two small feet.

"When the 'mothers' appeared on top with their escorts, the most daring climbers were already on the boulder, and the much loved and patient Kodak 'immortalized' them up there. How transitory seems human life, when one stands beside that marvelous rock that has probably stood there since time immemorial. How we enjoyed the view into the distance, hills, valleys, and fields where scarcely a hundred years ago the red man lived. It was a particular pleasure for us to enjoy all this with our friends, and with our mothers and Aunt Ida, with three valiant pioneer women, who had lived through the difficult time of settlement here in Texas and the war and Indian times. Their lives have been like a hard mountain climb, in our beloved Texas.

"But we turn our eyes back from the distant view to what is near at hand, and return to the cars for food and drink. Some of the relatives from the distant places had said, before we started the ascent, 'Is it safe to leave the food so near the road?', to which I answered, 'Here, in and near Fredericksburg, there is no danger.' And it was a relief to find everything undisturbed, for each one had brought back a good appetite and thirst from the climb.

"There must be some truth in the saying that mountaineers love liberty and respect the rights of others. Why? Mountaineers probably have to obey the laws of nature more closely than the inhabitants of the plains; in order not to fall, they must not be careless. That leads to self-respect; and with true, established self-respect comes the respect for others.

"Moreover, beauty has a powerful influence through its various forms: marvelous shapes of mountains and rocks, so many picturesque views of valleys, waterfalls, and heights. It leads us to observe the good and beautiful in our connection with human beings.

"The 'Balancing Rock' speaks a wonderful message, different to each one of us, yet it seems to me, one thing it can and must say to all: 'Stand firm whatever is supported, according to the law of balance; and may your life be well-balanced. Have only two points of support; live only for two principles: those of charity and truth.' The first includes respect for the good old customs, respect for and evaluation of the attainments of our ancestors, as well as regard for the coming generation. Only the sense of responsibility for our own actions in their relationship to the wholesome development of economical and political conditions can bring about that the human race exhibits a well-balanced whole. It can become that if the fundamental principles it observes are charity and truth, for truth includes all science, from physics to psychology.

"But all science is worthless without charity. So the Balancing Rock near Fredericksburg admonished us on August 17, 1924. And so I still could hear its speech while I ate my supper and enjoyed the security and freedom of Fredericksburg and its neighborhood. And joy remained with me, as we drove homeward, before the night veiled the lovely picture of Fredericksburg in darkness. The sight of the friendly houses to the right and left of the Cross Mountain, which lies in front of the town, in contrast with the green of the valleys and hills, tempted us to sing, and the music sounded through the valley, and echoed from the hills. It was a rarely so beautiful day."

In the summer of 1925 my sister and niece visited us on their return from Houston and Galveston, where they had been to visit my niece Hedwig Stanford and Aunt Ida Romberg, and where also Helene Romberg Mackensen, Brother Bernhard's only daughter, lives. Sister Bernhardine's son Rudolf Franke likewise lives there, and Julie Perlitz, who keeps house there for a cousin, Carl Perlitz (widower). Her sister Anna, also unmarried, lives with her mother in San Antonio. Julie and Anna are daughters of Carl and Friederike Perlitz. I should dearly like to have gone with them and seen these places again after eighty years. At that time, so I remember, one saw only wooden houses; now they tell me about large hotels, beautiful parks, resorts for tourists, and the large steamers which come up to Houston. Last year Daughter Louise was also there as delegate to a convention of the Eastern Star.

In August, 1926, we again spent several weeks at "Handy Stop," as Alfred Schnelle calls his home and place of business. In the dance hall, which at that time was being enlarged and which was finished, they gave a large opening celebration on a Sunday afternoon for which Daughter Louise and Niece Johanna had practiced the day before. They accompanied each other alternately on the piano, Johanna playing violin solos and Louise singing German songs. Singing societies from Comfort, Boerne, and Fredericksburg sang beautiful chorus numbers. In the evening free food was served to the singers, and afterwards there was a dance. It was marvelous how everything was accomplished, how smoothly everything went off. Only I must admit that the jazz music did not sound very harmonious to me,

A few days later Alfred Schnelle drove both of us, his mother, and Niece Frieda to Comfort to the Sons of Herman Home for the Aged, and so another of my wishes was fulfilled. A beautiful, quiet home the "aged" have up there on the steep hill, with a wonderful view into the distance. The next day the Stanfords from Houston surprised us with a visit; now four musical cousins were together. Johanna invited a mixed choir which she conducted, and they sang beautiful folksongs. Hedwig Stanford sang in her beautiful alto, and Louise sang solos.

In Fredericksburg we attended the Fair. The agricultural products interested me the most; the different grains were wonderfully arranged, and among them the different canned fruits.

Son Adolf, who takes his finest Angora goats to the Fair every year, met us there. On the same day we returned home, the Stanford family with us.

In July of the year 1927 Sister Lina, and her daughter Frieda came for a several weeks' visit, and Frieda and Louise began to copy my *Reminiscences*. At the same time, in August, for the third successive time, we again went to "Handy Stop," where we continued our writing.

On a rainy Sunday we visited the Fair, and we saw different acquaintances there in Fredericksburg, among them Willie Krueger and his wife from Twin Sisters. He told us about his father (which reminded me of days long past), who was now in Germany and there was having his memoirs printed in German and English (Max Krueger — 1851-1927 — Pioneer Life in Texas, 1930).

Many, many years ago his father, Max Krueger, came to Cypress Mill with a what was at that time very rare, photographic machine. One evening he and several neighbors had assembled at our house and were drinking wine (legal in those days). With animated conversation, interspersed with singing, the time passed quickly, and when they broke up, Mr. Krueger said, "I had not expected to have such a friendly, sociable evening in this lonely region!"

Lonely region!

Many may still, after sixty years, say that of our region, and yet, with the cars many people find their way here. Just recently, on Sunday, November 20, we experienced a great pleasure, for at Daughter Louise's suggestion several German-Americans came out here in their cars from Austin and presented a German play and a little operetta in our hall that had previously been presented to the Sons of Herman School. The singing teacher of the Conservatory of Music at the University also came along and sang several lovely songs in the English language.

I was especially pleased with what Mr. Max Werkenthin said about the preservation of the German language. He called Mr. Hermann Bohn a pillar of German culture. I also think we should make more effort to preserve our German language.

Through knowledge of the German language a spring of information is open to the student at the University, which can lead to important results in chemistry, mechanical engineering, natural science, and many other sciences; for it is a fact that the Germans have made important advances in these fields and have written technical books for many years. Before the War the Literary Digest once printed an article which stated that of all the inventions of the world, half were made by Germans, which at all events is a proof of their ability and progressiveness.

Well for those who realize this fact and are also good citizens of this land. All progress interests me. How everything has changed since I can remember! Time flies; it is no wonder that there are thousands and thousands of wheels turning, faster and always faster, on the earth, under it, in many places, and in the ships of the air. And all that electricity and the wireless telegraph have done for us! And photography in the last sixty years!

Sometimes all that is being done, all the accomplishments in various fields seem positively uncanny; and yet, long live Progress!

I hope this progress will render it possible for you children, grandchildren, and great-grandchildren of the Fuchs and Romberg families to have a family reunion on the Colorado River on the one-hundredth anniversary of the wedding of Grandfather and Grandmother, Adolf and Luise Fuchs, at the place where my dear parents-in-law forty-seven years ago on July 10, 1879, celebrated their golden wedding day in the circle of their children and grand-children and many dear friends. Since the Fuchs and Romberg families have known each other, they have been good, true friends, and therefore it would be a pleasure to me if they would join the descendants of the Grandparents Adolf and Luise Fuchs in the celebration in the year 1929.

How many descendants will there be in all? I still have nine living children, forty grandchildren, and thirty-three great-grandchildren. Years ago many relatives and friends enjoyed the hospitality in the home of my parents-in-law, in the romantic Colorado valley, and were welcome guests there. And if the dear grandparents were still living today, they would have a sympathetic, friendly word for each descendant and for their in-laws. So all of you come who can, and see the great-grandparents' place, where Sister-in-law Ulla's grandchild Armin Matern now lives. His father, Ino Matern, bought it from Albano Fuchs, Brother-in-law Hermann's son.

The old house is no longer standing, and only an old chimney marks the place, where once dear, peace-loving folks lived and where years ago my Wilhelm, your papa, greeted me when I first came into this region; where on the golden wedding day a large company assembled under a long arbor at an equally long table, and the grandparents received the homage of their friends, children, and grandchildren in words and song.

As proof of the long friendship between the Rombergs and Fuchses I am inserting this poem, which my father wrote for Father Fuchs' birthday, September 19, 1878:

If I could sing,
If I knew magic melodies,
O, then would I sing
To the clinking of the glasses,
Today on your birthday!

Would impressively compare you
To the tall live-oak,
That in olden days Towered toward Heaven,

Unharmed by storms of time.

Your children, your seed,
Joyfully they have flourished.
And always
By your side there stands
Your wife, your greatest fortune!

Not for gold did you aspire;
Only a quiet happy life
Was what you strove for
And what you achieved
Amidst this peaceful scene.

About you live your dear ones.
The sacred fire of music
Burns within your breast.
And the ever gracious Muses
Kindly shield the precious flame.

Demand no more of Life,
What better can you ask? Look above
And praise the gods,
That they have granted you so much.

May you and yours
Oft live this day again,
May you with song and music,
With clinking of your glasses,
Always find it, merry as today!

Now, your dear children, grandchildren and great-grandchildren, I should like to beg you to be especially thankful for your cousin Frieda Fuchs, as well as to Sister Louise ("Tante Lu"), that they arranged and copied what I have written down for you, and with my help have finished it; for with my eighty-seven years it would have been too hard for me to do alone.

The following short biography of your cousin was written by Daughter Dina:

Frieda Hermanna Fuchs was born on May 11, 1875, in the rough mountains on the Colorado River close to Marble Falls, in Burnet County, as the first child of her parents Hermann and Lina Fuchs, born Romberg. Her environment may have had something to do with the fact that she is of a romantic and poetical nature. She also inherited these qualities from her grandparents on both sides as well as from her father, who was very gifted as a writer.

But like her father she never enjoyed good health. As a child she suffered much, but always remained patient. On account of her health she was never able to attend school; but she always studied indefatigably, when her health allowed it, at home, with some help from her parents, but mostly alone through the reading of good literature.

At an early age she cultivated her talents, wrote for newspapers, and wrote poems, in all of which one could perceive her deep thought and feeling, as well as her noble and forgiving character that knew how to find the good and beautiful in everything.

After a severe illness in the year 1909, she became considerably stronger. She lived many years with her mother in San Antonio, took a training course in kindergarten, for which she was especially gifted, and taught several years. But as that also was too much for her strength, she moved with her mother to the home of her sister and brother-in-law in Kendall County, close to Fredericksburg. There on September 15, 1927, she married a friend of long standing, Leopold Flor, who also, like herself, likes to write poetry. May she be happy, for she has earned it!

Appendices

Mothers of the Nineteenth Century

(Written by Frieda H. Fuchs for the Fuchs and Romberg Family Reunion at Handy Stop, June 7, 1936)

Today we will give thought to some of the mothers of a hundred years ago, in the Fuchs and Romberg families, as we spoke more of our fathers at our other reunions, and because we know that the mother's influence is, as a rule, as great as that of the father. The information for this little talk I am getting from the book by Ottilie Fuchs Goeth, *Was Grossmutter Erzählt*, from the book *Erinnerungen*, by Louise Romberg Fuchs, and also from the recollections of Caroline Romberg Fuchs, who is with us today.

The Fuchs family landed at Galveston in January 1846. The Romberg family arrived there in November 1847.

The mother of our ancestor, pioneer Adolf Fuchs, was the third wife of Superintendent (Konrad Adolf) Fuchs at Güstrow, Germany, and he the fifth child was her only son and her pride. "He is my life," she once remarked in French, when the four-year-old boy with curly brown hair played near her in the garden.

By the way, it was the wife of her stepson, Fritz, to whom she made this remark. This stepson and family, too, came to Texas in later years. The youngest son of this family, Fritz Fuchs, lived at Cypress Mill, Texas, for many years. His wife, the sister of George Hoppe, was a good housekeeper and mother. Eleven children of theirs grew up to be useful citizens.

It is said that Adolf Fuchs inherited the musical talent from his mother. Her remark, "He is my life," may in part have referred to this musical talent of her son. And in later years, his songs have expressed her life, as for instance in his song, *Die Mutter Lullt den Knaben* ("Mother Sings Her Boy to Sleep").

Now let us know something of the mother of pioneer Adolf Fuchs' wife. Her maiden name was Helene Wien. Her father, a person of considerable wealth, was manager of some lands at the estate of the Countess Voss. Helene married Rümker, a prosperous merchant at Rostock. Luise Johanna Rümker, their second child, later became the wife of Adolf Fuchs. Luise Johanna was born October 14, 1809.

There is a picture of Helene Wien at the home of Max Goeth. This portrait Helene had intended to present to her husband upon his return from one of his trips to Spain. He exported Mecklenburg wheat to that country and imported Spanish wine. However, she thought the portrait was not a good likeness and put it away in a trunk, where it was found after her death. When her youngest child, Theodore, saw this picture, he cried out, "Mama." So it must have resembled her. At that time Luise was only four years old. She later said that she had never seen her father laugh any more after the death of her mother. When Luise was twelve years old, her father suddenly died and left no will. It is said that for this reason his four children lost much of their property. Yet all received a good education. In the family of Hermann Fuchs are still the books by Schiller, which Helene Rümker received as a present from her husband during the first year of their marriage.

When grown, Luise Johanna Rümker and her younger sister, Ulrike, visited their Uncle Rümker at

Güstrow. Here Luise first met Adolf Fuchs, when he and a friend, who was a relative of the Rümker family, came home from their studies at a university. Of this time pioneer Adolf Fuchs tells in a song which he wrote and composed, *Lieder Ohne Worte und Ohne Melodie* which may be translated, "Song Without Words and Without Melody." Adolf and Louise married July 10, 1829. They first lived at Waren for six years, where Adolf Fuchs held a position as Lutheran minister. They were transferred to Kölzow, and he had charge of the congregation. Luise still had enough property from her father to furnish her home beautifully; and as she was rather delicate, she always had help to assist her in her housework. Here in Texas her daughters and later her oldest granddaughters helped her much with the housework. In spite of delicate health, she was a good housekeeper and cook, and she had the splendid gift of making the plainest log cabin seem cheerful and homelike. A bouquet of flowers, autumn leaves, or sprigs of grass, were always in her room. Her children would bring home to her when returning from their work, hunting, or even Indian scouting, anything they found that they thought would be of interest to her. She was always a kind companion to her children; and for everyone who came to their home, she had a kind thought and word. For her grandchildren she had a "toy box" containing many toys of various forms and material. All those who played with them surely remember this toy box. But best of all they remember her, the kind little grandmother, whom they thought the most beautiful and dearest in all the world.

While the Fuchs family was still living at Cat Springs in Austin County, many immigrants as well as neighbors came, to whom hospitality was extended and assistance was given. How many names do I remember which my father, Hermann Fuchs, has mentioned! Among these early friends were Dr. Nagel, whose son, Charles Nagel, wrote A Boy's Civil War Story[1], and many, many others who have been prominent in the affairs of the State.

In November 1847 it was when the immigrant Johannes Christlieb Nathanael Romberg and family stopped at the home of Adolf Fuchs in Cat Springs to get information in regard to roads leading to the former's place on the San Bernardo. And the friendship between these two families dates from this time.

Before getting acquainted with Johannes Christlieb Nathanael Romberg's wife, Friederike, we first want to know something of his mother, Friederike. Her maiden name was Conradine Sophie Friederike Hast. Her father was a well-to-do Lutheran pastor. The daughter's wish was to get the same education as her brothers, who attended a university. But her father was opposed to it. So she had one of her brothers to instruct her; besides, secured books to study by herself. Astronomy was her favorite study, and for this subject she got a map of the stars. This map has in later years often been used by her son, grandchildren, and great-grandchildren.

In 1807 she married Bernhard Friedrich Christlieb Romberg, a pastor of the Lutheran Church. Johannes Christlieb Nathanael Romberg was their only child. This son too was anxious to get a university education; but on account of weak eyes, he could not study as much as he wished. It therefore was decided that he should become a merchant; thus in the home of Johannes Dietrich Bauch, a merchant at Schwerin, Johannes Christlieb Nathanael Romberg as apprentice met his future wife Friederike. So both women who meant more to him than any others in the world had the name of Friederike. Friederike Romberg was born August 14, 1812, as one of the younger daughters of the merchant Dietrich Bauch and his wife Dorothea. After her father's death her mother continued the business. She was an energetic

---

1 Available in Texianer Verlag

and practical woman and managed the business successfully, thus supporting the household and giving her children an education. Friederike was the only one among her sisters who had no musical talent and could not sing or play a musical instrument; but evidently the law of compensation in nature provided her with superior intelligence and love for books and learning. She became a governess with her fourteenth year. This was after she had met Johannes Romberg in her mother's business and had often read to him. The two had become the best of friends and had promised each other to wait for the time when they could become married, when they were older and Johannes had a business of his own.

As a governess her life was not always easy. At one place the pupils, about as old and taller than she, liked to tease her whenever they found out that she had received a letter from Johannes Romberg. At another place she had to be the peacemaker between the parents of her pupils upon request of one or the other. However, after seven or eight years of hard work for both, young Friederike and Johannes married in 1833 and lived at Boizenburg, where he had established himself as merchant. He never was fond of the merchant's business, and this may have been one of the many reasons why he realized the wish to come to Texas. Friederike Romberg taught her children here in Texas.

The grandmother, Friederike, who stayed in Mecklenburg, often sent good books and many other presents, toys for the younger children, things to wear, candy, dried fruit, flower seed, jewelry, and so on. Her youngest daughter, Caroline Bauch, often stayed with the lonely grandmother and would read, sing, and play the piano for her.

Later when Caroline also came to Texas together with her mother, two brothers, and sister Louise, she often spoke of the happy days she had spent with the grandmother of whom she said, "She was an exceptionally fine woman."

Johannes and Friederike lived very happily together. In their home in Fayette County, the mother read to the family in the evenings from German, French, or English books. She translated fluently without stopping for a preliminary reading. All this time she would be knitting, too. She was not only the teacher in the family, she was also the bookkeeper and a good housekeeper, knowing how to prepare and preserve food. Above all, she was wonderful companion to her husband.

In this the two pioneer mothers, Fuchs and Romberg, have been equally great. Each was to her husband a fine, understanding companion. Each husband has appreciated this companionship. The one has expressed it in verse; the other also in song.

And here we are their descendants: teachers, doctors, musicians—Oscar Fox, the composer—artists, and the important ranchmen and farmers, too. Each descendant everywhere fills his useful place in the community and in the state. And if there are only a few who have reached near the top in any special line, most of us have "climbed" for a full life, for our family, and our Texas.

In closing I wish to say this of our two pioneer mothers: both saw more clearly than their husbands the importance of a good education for their children. Lovers of freedom and of ideal home life, the husbands were contented in their home, in the free young Texas with its possibilities for each person who wished to work. The wives saw that unlimited freedom can only be preserved for individuals as well as for nations in course of time and with growth of population if knowledge is possessed by the people. They realized that, besides building good characters, it was a primary duty of parents to impart knowledge to their children, as much as the pioneer conditions would permit. For this foresight I honor our pioneer mothers. They have tried to live up to this conviction as best they could under unaccustomed surroundings and daily duties, and hindered much by their frail health.

A white flower to these pioneer mothers,
 two,
In honor of their brave deeds and ideals true.
And a flower to many, many others
Of our kind and brave pioneer mothers.

Reminiscences of Theodora Hoppe Fuchs

(Mrs. Fritz Fuchs) Written down on July 19, 1930
Translated from the German by Theodora Goebel Rantz

Herewith I shall try to give a fairly accurate account of our lives together since we have been married now for over sixty-one years. After we had been engaged for several months without knowing each other very well, it was March 2, 1869 when Grandfather Fuchs [Pastor Adolf Fuchs] married us at George Stolley's [second husband of Sophie Julia Schroeter, the second wife and widow of Hans Adolf Hoppe] at nine o'clock in the evening.

Thus on the 25th of March Grandfather Fuchs took us in his big horse wagon over to his old home on the river, where we spent the first night, and then the next day they took us to Pecan Creek where Papa lived, as he was herding sheep on the halves there for Aunt Ulla Matern.

When we arrived there, I found everything very dreary and desolate. As is usual in such a bachelor household, there wasn't much furniture. The entire furnishings consisted of a small table which he and Julius Romberg had made themselves from good walnut wood, right well made. Then Papa had a chest, which he probably had made himself, too, for his few belongings. The bed consisted of several sheep pelts, a feather sack and a quilt on the floor.

For cooking and baking there was the fireplace in the room, in which we cooked and baked our food in an iron frying pan and a bacon pan. To cook we had, so to say, nothing except cornbread and meat of all kinds. Especially much venison was eaten since Papa shot so many deer which were so plentiful at that time. Also, fish were caught in great numbers since we lived so near the Colorado River. Wild hogs were shot, too. Thus one had enough to eat to live.

After we had been there a few days, a bed had to be seen to. So Papa went to the Cypress saw mill, and there he made an immense bedstead out of old cypress wood, and brought it home in old Fuchs' wagon. I didn't like it at all as it was made of poor lumber, and then it was much too large for my woolen mattress, which I brought with me. There wasn't much that I brought with me, mostly just a pair of pillows and a few quilts. My trousseau was very small since we had used up pretty well everything during the war. Anyway, we lived on very little so that my step-mother never even thought of getting anything special for me. We lived so very poorly.

In these limited circumstances we lived on, really quite comfortably. Papa tended the sheep for it was lambing time. The sheep had to be sheared, too, and we received half of the wool as well as half of the lambs. We also kept a shepherd for a while, a Negro boy, to herd the lambs. I often helped with the herding; I had nothing else to do. We had a small garden down on the creek. I also tried to raise a few chicks. Aunt Ulla left me a few hens. There were also a few bee-hives to supply us with honey. We caught some new swarms, too.

That year Ulrich Varnhagen's mother [Adolfine/Ino Fuchs, daughter of Pastor Adolf Fuchs] died when he was born, and we moved to [Adolf] Varnhagen's for a while to do the house work for him. Aunt Ulla [Ulrike Fuchs Matern] took the child. She lived near her parents near the river. Later we moved back to Pecan Creek, where Minna was born [1870]. That was in 1870, and that year we moved to Cypress. We lived a few months at Aunt Louise and Uncle Wilhelm Fuchs' home. But before we moved to Cypress (it probably was the first year), Papa made a trip to Industry, where he received his inheritance from his father's (Fritz Fuchs, half-brother of Pastor Adolf Fuchs) estate. I think it was $300. The place sold for $600, of which his brother received half. While he was away, Helene Matern [daughter of Ulrike/Ulla Fuchs Matern] stayed with me. She was always so jolly, and her brothers and sisters came over to visit her there.

When we were living at Cypress and left Uncle Wilhelm's, we bought a place from Mr. Crosby and moved there. We took the sheep there and from then on started sheep raising. We also bought several old cows, and Uncle Wilhelm gave us one; from that we got a herd of cattle started, and in a few years we had s small bunch of cattle. I even sold butter in those days, for Mr. Grate and Mr. Sultemeier were living the bachelor's life on the Pedernales, and they always came to me for butter.

We lived there at Cypress until about 1874. Bettie was born there [1872], also Julia [1874]. We had a shepherd there, a cripple with a wooden leg. Papa often helped out at the mill for Mr. Geiger.

In the fall of 1874 we moved to the Pedernales into a small three-room house that Papa and another young man built there. Here in November [1875] little Emma was born. Here too we had shepherds, first Mr. —, then Moritz Goebel, and later Heinrich Ullrich. In this little house Emil too was born [1876] after the poor little Emma had been dead one year. Two years later [1878] Fritz was born in this same house, a short while before we moved into the big rock house, which had just been finished. I carried him over there when he was eleven or twelve days old. Yes, in those days we had pretty good luck with sheep and cattle. Lots of hogs were raised then, too. Gradually, Papa bought more land, so that the ranch got larger and larger; in those days much land also was used for sheep that did not belong to us.

Gradually the children grew up, and many more were born, too. In the rock house Gini was born in 1880, Anna in 1883, later Olga [1885], then George [1887]; and after George the little Matilda, but who lived only six weeks before she died [1889/1890?]. All the other children also became sick; then Uncle Benno Fuchs [Benjamin F. Fuchs, son of Pastor Adolf Fuchs] went for a doctor in Blanco. He soon had them all well again.

Oh yes, before we moved from Cypress, I received a small inheritance from my father's (Hans Adolf Hoppe) estate. I don't remember how much. I received a team of horses, I know. Papa traded one of them off for a load of corn. The other one became our only saddle horse. His name was "Werder." Papa once had a horse, but it died for him one day when he rode it to Richter's [Johann Rudolph Eduard Richter?]. He came home with the saddle on his back. How much else I received from my father's estate I don't remember, but it seems to me we paid off the place at Cypress with it. In those days I paid no attention to money matters. As a child and young girl I never had a cent in my hand. I suppose that is why I never in my life paid any attention to money matters—foolishly.

While we were living on the Pedernales, the children grew up. First Minna and Bettie, who had to attend to much already, had to help with the lambs, for instance. Probably they helped with the cattle, too. Papa never interested himself in cattle, only in sheep and hogs. At that time we had a nice herd of cattle. During the eighties Papa bought eighty head of cattle, mostly cows with heifer calves, from Mr. Smith, who lived with us then, and we paid him for the cattle by boarding him for many years. We also had many renters—first the old Gruppes lived down there in the little house. Later, a family Davis, then Ernst Goeth, Charlie's parents. He taught school then for our children and his. When he left, Mercedes' [daughter-in-law, wife of Fritz, Jr.) Grandmother [Maria Schroeter Stuckert?] lived there and taught the children. Then we had Dose as renter, later Rothenberg.

Old Mr. Stolley also lived with us a while. We also had Professor Wartensleben and his two children, Max and Lottie.

Yes, the children grew up. Emil and Fritz had to attend to the cattle since they were small and they were still at home.

Theodora Fuchs
July 19, 1930

At Grandfather's by Helene Romberg Mackensen

Will you join me this morning for a short visit to my childhood land of memory? I am on my way to Grandfather's. We will walk up the hill together and turn in at the rough-hewn gate in the corner of the fence. Our path leads us part a rosebush with dark red velvety roses, up to the old log house. Just in front of the gallery, on each side of the walk is a trellis overgrown with Madeira vine, fragrant with lacy, white blossoms, and with roses that grow in clusters and shade from the faintest pink into dark red, some even into blue. We step from the gallery with its sand-floor into the wide hall connecting the two log houses. The floor of the hall is of red cedar, worn uneven with long use, the knots in the wood forming little hills as the softer wood around them has worn away. Many times during the summer the relatives would gather in this hall for a happy social time. To the right is Grandfather's room. Here he spent most of his time. I can see him plainly now, sitting over a chess-game, with perhaps Uncle Johannes, Uncle Julius, Uncle Hermann or Heinrich Franke—Grandfather with his long white hair and beard, smoking a long pipe. These chess games lasted for hours and, if begun in the morning, would be often continued after dinner. The players entered into them with all their might; and sitting motionless each would study how he might get the best of his opponent. So we will let them play and turn to the left toward the kitchen.

To the left of the kitchen-door is a small table with a sandstone top, which Uncle Johannes made. The water bucket has its place there, also the washboard, and the turtle shell, bleached white with age, which holds the soap. To the right is a pantry with its door of slats through which one could peep at the bags and boxes and dishes on the shelves, wondering what might be in them. As it is almost dinner-time, we will have a look at the kitchen. It is lighted by a long, low window in the south which slides open all the way when it is pushed. It was on the fireplace in the back of the room that Grandmother and her daughters prepared the meals before our modern iron stoves came into use. I do not know what we will have to eat today, but I am sure there will be some smoked beef. Tante Ida used to slice a big hunk of it, big as your arm on a hard board. That board, by the way, is still in use at cousin Hedwig Stanford's and brings up memories of good things to eat every time I see it. We may have ambrosia, too — Götterspeise, we used to call it, made of fruit and crumbled rye bread with thick cream, and finally cinnamon sprinkled over all of it. Perhaps we will eat some of those big yellow clingstone peaches from Grandfather's orchard back of the house.

And now we will go to Grandfather's room; and while he and his partner finish their game of chess, we will take a look at the room. It is rather large, not very high, the beams in the ceiling showing dark against the freshly whitewashed background. Up over the door a shelf crowded with books runs the whole length of the room. I often wonder why it was up so high. Perhaps because books, though always precious, were especially so almost a hundred years ago when that shelf was put there, high up, out of harm's way. Grandfather thought a great deal of his books. In fact, he looked upon them as a necessity of life and used to call reading matter nourishment. An encyclopedia, Shakespeare, Dickens, Goethe, Schiller and other classical works found their places up there. A wardrobe and some more shelves occupied the space below. In the center of the north wall stood the dresser. Above it, the clock (the same one now rests peacefully in my attic), a bed, one on each side of the dresser.

There was a small square window near the south-east corner of the room where Grandfather's table stood. He usually sat in the home-made rocker in front of it. Some inexperienced hand had evidently fashioned this chair out of green wood, for it is quite warped. The runners are of about four-inch boards and accompany any effort at rocking with a kind of knotty little tune. When it was first made, it served as a cradle for Uncle Julius, long years ago.

When Grandfather smoked and mused about something he was writing, he sat in that chair. The writing was first done on a slate with slate pencil. Sometimes that pencil would get dull, then Grandfather would sharpen it by rubbing it on the edge of the table, gradually wearing grooves. into the wood. We grandchildren used to marvel at these grooves and admire them according to their depth. When the writing was finished, Grandfather would usually copy it in ink at a small desk that was so high that he had to stand before it. The ink he used was not the ink you buy in a store, but ink he made himself out of those brown balls that are occasionally found on the leaves of oak trees.

When his pipe went out, Grandfather took a Fidibus from the holder on the table, and then turned around to light it at the stove just back of him. A fidibus is a strip of paper folded like the bias tape mothers use to bind the armholes in their children's underwear. A supply was made out of old letters or from the pages cut out of an old copy-book. We used to make a bundle of them for Grandfather's birthday, and found it quite hard to cut and fold them evenly.

But I must tell you about the stove and queer old drum over it. This drum was a part of the stove pipe and helped to keep the room warm. It looked like a small barrel closed up, but a hole like a stove pipe went through the length of it. Grandfather baked an apple there once in a while just as is done in the German stories you read.

Grandfather liked fun, too. Occasionally he would make little jig-saw puzzles that we all enjoyed. He could cut up a square or triangle or some other shape of pasteboard into a few more triangles, squares and oblong pieces in such a way that it would take you a long time to put them together again.

For a last look at the old place that has changed altogether, let me take you to the back yard where the old walnut tree with spreading branches stood. We children romped in its shade and ate the nuts while the grown folks sat quietly chatting. Finally the old tree died and Uncle Johannes made a bookcase out of its solid trunk. Cousin Hedwig Stanford has it in her home, and probably some of the old books from Grandfather's high shelf are resting still behind its doors.

Written for the Romberg reunion at Barton Spring, Austin, summer of 1936, by Helene Romberg Mackensen. The place described was at Black Jack Springs, Fayette County, Texas.

Biographical Sketch

(Introduction to the collected, published poems of Johannes Romberg: *Gedichte von Johannes Romberg*. Dresden und Leipzig: E. Piersons Verlag, 1900.)

Johannes Christlieb Nathanael Romberg was born on November 10, 1808, in Alt Bukow in Mecklenburg-Schwerin, where his father was a pastor.

He spent a happy childhood and received his first instruction from a tutor in the company of two boy cousins and a girl cousin. Later on he visited the school in Alt Bukow. Shortly before his death, his father stood bail for a friend and in the process lost the entire fortune which had been his wife's dowry. That was a severe blow for the family, and not alone because of lack of funds, but also because of an eye ailment incurred while getting a haircut, young Romberg had to forego his passionately loved studies. That same eye ailment, which necessitated his spending half a year in a dark room, brought him an antipathy for haircuts which he remembered his whole life long.

For this reason the poet continually wore long, curly flowing hair until his final days. Since he had to master an occupation, he chose the merchant's trade without feeling any inclination for it. Toward this end he entered the business firm of Herr Johannes Dietrich Bauch in Schwerin. In order to escape the dry side of the calling, he took up literary studies with his future wife, the daughter of that merchant.

His fiancee read aloud to him, and later they discussed the theme being dealt with. The books for which Herr Johannes Romberg had the most preference were the works of Homer, Schiller, Goethe, Shakespeare,

Wieland, and Jean Paul, to which Gustav Freitag was also included later.

By preference the youthful poet occupied himself with astronomical studies. His mother had already had a great preference for astronomy. Without preliminary studies she searched through books she had acquired to orient herself about the science of the stars. Her intellectually exciting life greatly influenced her son, whose future wife often assured her children, "I count her among the good women, who do honor to mankind."

In 1833 Romberg established a business in Boizenburg, where he found a faithful friend in the Rector, Reinhard, there.

In the same year he also married the daughter of his employer, Friederike Amalia Elise Bauch.

In order to offer a better capability of existence to his children, of which nine were born to him and one of them died at a most tender age, he formulated the plan to emigrate to the state of Texas lying in western North America—a decision which he carried out in 1847. He traveled with his family over New Orleans to Galveston, the main port of Texas, in order to go from there into the interior.

He bought a farm on the San Bernard River and set up farming and cattle raising, making the beautiful words of the old master Goethe his principle in life:

> *Work by day, in the evening guests,*
> *Weeks of toil, happy feats.*

Stimulating evenings were spent in association with the neighbors of that time, the main contingent of whom were produced by the educated Germany of the period.

Since there were neither schools nor teachers in Texas, in those days, the poet instructed his children himself. The post office was ten miles from his farm, and he had to pay a gold dollar for the first letter which be received from his mother. Conditions then were very primitive. Boards weren't available, and therefore, the poet lived with his family in a log cabin whose floor was never covered. Indeed, as the poet in later years often asserted in family circles and among friends, he was very happy and satisfied during his six first years in his log cabin. Peace-loving by nature, he took pride in reconciling circles of neighbors who sometimes opposed one another with hostility.

He had a strong dislike for all business matters and left those sorts of things to his wife. However, he insisted that his debts were paid, not just when money was often very scarce in his first years here, but also during the Civil War.

A most intense feeling of justice and a most scrupulous conscientiousness conquered the amiable poet. He was no friend of raucous conviviality, but he had his own preference for conversations and rather small parties. He understood very well how to lure out a person and to move him to express his best thoughts and views. Even with those who stood far beneath him intellectually, his conversations were quite interesting.

Of small stature and unassuming manner, he was one of the friendliest figures in the growing colonies in this region at that time. He never used to pass unkind judgment on others, and he often said to his daughter-in-law, the wife of his son Bernhard, "We may blame others only out of self-defense or love."

A loving father, he was exceedingly anxious in regard to his children and could become very uneasy if one of them occasionally stayed out late. Then he reprimanded the expected one to his wife. Now when the rebuked child finally came home and his wife told him to deliver the scolding to the proper address, as a rule he would say, "There he is now!" and he was satisfied.

In the family circle he liked harmless pranks and droll teasing, and there was much joking at the very lively table.

"I often remember," so related Mrs. Bernhard Romberg, "observing with a kind of child's astonishment his wandering up and down, and how he, moreover, had a word of teasing or a caress for each of his children, who were gathered around the long table."

In the summer, however, the short rest hour in the evenings was regularly spent outdoors. Then there were discussions about astronomy, the position, revolution, and relationships of the heavenly bodies to one another, and the laws by which the stars moved in their orbits were investigated.

Discussions were frequently held about poetry and philosophy. For the most part politics stayed out of the picture, for he was no friend of disagreeable conversations. In the long winter evenings his wife read aloud, and with preference something from Goethe and Lessing was chosen. To the extent that it was decent, a lighter tonic was also chosen from time to time. On the long board above the door, from wall to wall, stood his greatest treasure, his cherished collection of books, of which the encyclopedia and the classics made up the most part.

While his children were growing up, at his suggestion around 1857 there arose a literary club among the young people of the small circle, which received the name "Prairie Flower," and whose origin Romberg greeted with these words:

> *Blümelein,*
> *Zart and klein,*
> *Wünscht dir gutes Wetter,*
> *Mögst gedeihn*
> *Auf texanischer Prairie.*
> *Prosa deuten deine Blätter,*
> *Deine Blüten Poesie.*

Biographical Sketch

(Little flower,
Small and tender,
Wish you good weather,
May you flourish
On the Texas prairie.
Prose signify your leaves,
Your blossoms poetry.)

To all of them, who took part in those literary amusements in those days, that time is everlastingly remembered as a passage from a charming poem of youth. He himself had produced some of his most beautiful poems for it and with them offered a forceful stimulus to those efforts. He often teased his children during these occasions, when he sometimes dealt with their materials, in another form, of course. In those years since he had been in Black Jack Springs, he also founded a reading club, which now and then brought fresh reading matter into that remote region.

The Civil War came and tore everything apart with its horrors for a few years. Since Romberg was too old to be eligible to be drafted into the army of the Confederacy, which was fighting for slavery, he stayed quietly at home while two of his sons held out in Central America and California since they didn't want to fight for the Confederacy. Often for long periods of time, and once even for nine months, there was no definite news from his sons, and during this time the poet was in an abnormally irritable mood.

Several years after the close of the Civil War, German newspapers brought news of the declaration of war between France and Germany, and Romberg stated, "Now the Frank again thrusts his sword onto the scale of justice," and then in the course of the conversation he added, "Yes, if I could provide Germany with victory, I would gladly give up my harvest." That was to mean much to the weak, cautious person, to whom that was not just an expression. According to his means, he participated vigorously in the collections for Germany's soldiers, which were set going here.

In his old days yet he often went to his daughter-in-law and brought along a poem or even from time to time a rather large notebook with a story in verse and then said, "Yes, Lining, that is nothing great, but you know, I can't do anything right any more, and I do want to do something. Will you read that, please?"

In 1883 his wife died. The then seventy-five year-old man missed her a great deal, and he never got over her loss. After her death, he felt himself getting lonelier and lonelier. And only in the circle of his family and in nature, which he cherished, did he get away from his sorrow to some extent.

In his eighty-second year of life Johannes Romberg died of a stroke on February 6, 1891. With him the German colony lost very much, for his intellectually stirring life was beneficial to all the groups surrounding him, and his refreshing humor won over all hearts to him.

He was a brilliant testimony to the activity of Germans in other lands. Like the gnarled oak in his homeland, he showed a bold front to all of fortune's storms and without flinching bravely followed his course and had more beneficial effects in small circles than many others did in large ones.

In most of his deeply-felt songs, especially the hymns of spring, he imitated nature surrounding him and sang his songs to his friends without thinking of their being publicized.

Although the son of a pastor, he represented completely the naturalistic world view, and he constantly tried to find life's sunny sides, following the words of his contemporary, the farmer-philosopher Konrad Deubler, who says so appropriately,

"Every day of our life should be a festival, and every hour in the day should be the greatest highlight."

May his poems win friends among the children of the German homeland, which he loved and revered so unspeakably.

Alfred Wagner
Translated by Kenneth W. Fuchs

Johannes Christlieb Nathanael Romberg
German Poet Of Texas

By Selma Metzenthin-Raunick

In The *Collection of Johannes Romberg's poetry* edited by Alfred Wagner (E. Pierson's Verlag, Dresden and Leipzig, 1900), we read in the last stanza of the introductory poem the following self-appraisal:
>Zwar es kann ein grosser Chor
>Nicht den Wald durchdringen,
>Aber für ein lauschend Ohr
>Bleibt es doch ein Singen.

Again we read in Romberg's philosophical poem, *Genie and Talent*, this modest classification of himself:
>Wir kleinen Leute sind zufrieden
>Mit dem was uns die Muse bringt.
>Das Grosse ist uns nicht beschieden,
>Wir freu'n uns, wenn ein Vers gelingt.

Johannes Romberg's judgment of his own poetry is too modest. In pleasing unaffected style and with complete mastery of poetic form, he interprets life as he feels and sees it.

Johannes Romberg is not the only outstanding German poet of Texas. A few may perhaps be said to have surpassed him in certain qualities. There were, for example, Pedro Ilgen, a clergyman who spent a number of years in Texas (mainly in the town of Yoakum); Ferdinand Lohmann of Comfort; Hulda Walter of Fredericksburg, the first native Texan writing German verse; and Clara Matthäi ("Gertrud Hoff") of Bellville, another native Texan. Pedro Ilgen has given us some poetry of more depth and grandeur in his religious verse and in his poems on the First World War. Ferdinand Lohmann has written with greater fervor and eloquence his exhortations to the German pioneers to remember their mission, i.e., to contribute of the best of the old fatherland – home-making, music, a keen appreciation of responsibility—and to accept only the best in the new homeland. Hulda Walter, who, like Romberg, composed much regional poetry, employs a loftier language, gives more spiritualized images. Clara Matthäi, like Romberg, wrote much lyric poetry and sometimes surpasses the latter in the musical quality of her verse. And there were other writers from whom we have occasionally some exceptional gem of poetry. But there are only two poets, Clara Matthäi and Hulda Walter, whose compositions are of the same consistent merit as Romberg's. And there is not one of our German Texas poets who equaled him in variety of subject matter, of form and metre. Several of Romberg's longer narrative poems, as well as a few shorter ones and one or two lyrics, are written in blank verse. Each poem seems to be poured into its own appropriate form. We find in Romberg's compositions lyric, narrative, and dramatic poetry—pastorals, romances, and brief dramas.

Much of Romberg's poetry is philosophical. Like many of the European emigrants of the early nineteenth century who were influenced by the French Revolution, Johannes Romberg was irreligious and even somewhat antagonistic toward the church. Still, he confesses that there is much we humans do not know and merely "ahnen" (divine) and that there is a Great Spirit beyond our erring intellect and scientific reasoning:

> *Wer steigt hinab bis zu der Quelle,*
> *Woraus das Dasein strömt and springt,*
> *Woraus das Leben Well' auf Welle*
> *Durchs unermess'ne Weltall dringt?*

Wer dringt zur Quelle der Bewegung,
Wer zu der Kraft verborg'nem Sitz.
Wer zu des Geistes erster Regung,
Zu des Bewusstseins erstem Blitz?

Wir können irren nur and träumen,
Wir sehen nicht der Wahrheit Strahl,
Doch in des Herzens heil'gen Räumen
Wohnt still ein hohes Ideal.

Das ist das Gute and das Schöne,
Das Göttliche, das in uns lebt,
Und das uns arme Erdensöhne
Hoch über Staub and Stoff erhebt.

Der Philosoph baut sein System
Doch selbst mit Wissenschaft verbunden
Löst er nicht auf das Weltproblem,
Den Schlussstein hat er nie gefunden.

Was uns umgiebt, das ist Natur,
Die Welten laufen ihre Bahnen,
Wir können tief im Herzen nur,
Den Gott, den Quell des Daseins ahnen.

Und unser Herz ist auch Natur,
Kann es uns eine Lüge sagen
Wenn wir des grossen Geistes Spur
Im All der Welt zu ahnen wagen?

We find a touch of fine humor in Romberg's poetry which does not hesitate to create a laugh at himself or to include himself. An unusually clever piece of humor is his spring song, *Gefährlich*, which points out the natural dangers of that season, and his dramatic narrative, Der Teufel and der Dichter, in which Satan loses his wager to the poet rather than to be obliged to listen to the latter's poetry.

Romberg's poems of spring have a soft nostalgic note, not usually found in the author's compositions. It is in spring that his beloved wife died; this tragedy colors all his later spring poetry. So he writes the first spring following his wife's death:

> *Seh ich auch die Frühlingsfeier*
> *Und des Werdens schöne Zeit,*
> *Deckt sich doch ein dunkler Schleier*
> *Ueber all die Herrlichkeit.*

And again, three years later:

> *Zwar die Wunde vernarbt, die damals so*
> *heftigt geschmerzt hat,*
> *Doch die Erinnerung bleibt, and noch ist*
> *kein Tag mir vergangen*
> *Dass ich nicht ihrer gedacht. Das Leben*
> *ist öde geworden...*

Perhaps the most striking of Romberg's "home" poetry is *Idyll*, which brings to mind Goethe's *Hermann and Dorothea*. It is an attractive picture of the home of a pioneer family. The opening lines carry us to Texas, the crude bench under the wide-spreading, shade-giving live oak with its permanent green and picturesque hanging moss; so dear to Texans.

> *Unter der Lebenseich', wo selbst am*
> *heissesten Mittag,*
> *Wenn kein Blatt sich bewegt, das leise*
> *Säuseln des Zephyrs*
> *Nimmer ruht, und die Sonne sich*
> *vergeblich bestrebet,*
> *Durch das dichte Gezweig in den tiefen*
> *Schatten zu dringen,*
> *Hier am eichnen Tisch auf Sesseln von*
> *Brettern gefertigt,*

> *Sass mit der Freundin vertieft im Gepräche*
> *über Europa Ida…*

Again we join the simple meal of the pioneer family, which, in spite of its simplicity of living, has not quite given up earlier refinements:

> *Auf des Tischzeugs Weisse und auf die*
> *silbernen Löffel*
> *Goss sein schimmerndes Licht von Osten,*
> *der steigende Vollmond.*

Romberg, like the majority of educated Germans of his time, was a complete individualist and a passionate defender of personal liberty. To see even an animal deprived of its freedom aroused his compassion. In the last stanza of his poem *Vogel im Bauer*, he has these characteristic lines:

> *Riegle auf des Kerkers Pforte*
> *Gieb ihm seine Welt zurück,*
> *Gieb ihm Freiheit. In den Worte*
> *Liegt ein unaussprechlich Glück.*

One of Romberg's most tender lyrics was decicated to a bird which came to its end shot by a young lad:

> *Und endlich kam der Frühling auch,*
> *Belebte alles wieder,*
> *Das Vöglein sass auf gruenem Strauch*
> *Und sann auf neue Lieder.*

> *Es fuehlte in der kleinen Brust*
> *Des Daseins ganze Wonne,*
> *Und wärmte sich voll Lebenslust*
> *Im Strahl der goldnen Sonne.*

Bald flog es auf zu einem Baum
Besah der Knospen Fülle,
Die, bald erwacht vom Wintertraum,
Zersprengen ihre Hülle.

Schon übt es sich ein Liedlein ein,
Das es im Chor will singen,
Wenn aller Vögel Melodein
In Feld and Wald erklingen.

Doch ach, ein Knabe schlich daher
Der zielt and zielet wieder,
Und schiesst mit seinem Mordgewehr
Den kleinen Vogel nieder.

We might expect to find among Romberg's productions poems of Sehnsucht for the fatherland, poems expressing disappointment in the new home. But there is practically nothing of depression or dissatisfaction. Even when his verse reports a sad event, Romberg ends his narrative on a cheerful note. Romberg accepted life as it was. Only one or two of his poems are reminiscent of the fatherland. One poem, however, *Vineta*, suggests that perhaps the harmonious and happy Johannes Romberg also held, deep within himself, some vague, unsatisfied Sehnsucht.

There were several political events in his fatherland which inspired Romberg to poetic expression—especially, the German victory over France in 1871 and the death of Emperor William I.

Johannes Romberg composed long narrative poems dealing with family-life, of similar style as his shorter *Idyll*. These have not yet been published.

Romberg wrote two brief dramas based on German legends—*Ein kleines Bruchstück von einem grossen Epos* and *Rübezahl*. The latter presents the legendary figure of the Silesian Mountains, Rübezahl, who plays mischievous pranks on human folk, but occasionally helps a deserving person in distress. Both the brief Fragment and Rübezahl show the same poetic feeling and skill as Romberg's simpler verse. As far as I know, not one of the other Texas poets, except the late Professor Sibbern of Texas Luthern College, who composed a number of classical plays published in Germany, tried his hand extensively at serious drama. About 1936, F. Neuhäuser, editor of the Freie Presse of San Antonio, published a short play, *Die Pioniere*.

Johannes Christlieb Nathanael Romberg (1808-1891, although not a native Texan—he came from Alt Bukow in Mecklenburg-Schwerin, in 1847—lost no time in "planting both feet in Texas soil." How thoroughly he identified himself with Texas is shown in his poetry, of which more than half would come under the category of regional. There is no sentimental nostalgic verse, no emphasis on advantages left behind. Romberg lived in the present. He was filled with the determination to overcome all difficulties that might be encountered and to build a happy home-life for his family.

There were indeed many difficulties to overcome when the Rombergs arrived in Galveston. They had left a comfortable, cultured home to dwell now in a two-room log-cabin with a garret to which the children climbed by means of the high back of a bench which the poet had constructed. In fact, the poet, assisted by his brother, had built the entire cabin and some of the furnishings. He was very fond of cabinet-making and all sorts of carpentering and building.

Romberg's father was a Lutheran pastor, and the son would have studied theology had his weak eyes not prevented this. It was decided that Johannes go into business. He received training in the business house of his father-in-law, then set up a retail store of his own in Boizenburg-an-der-Elbe. But he disliked his work very much; in fact, he disliked all business transactions and the handling of money. He would have preferred to take up a trade like carpentry or cabinetmaking, but at that time such a calling was considered unsuited for one of his social standing. Johannes then made carpentry his avocation, observing master carpenters and practising with saw and chisel and whatever tools he possessed. This stood him in good stead in his later life in Texas.

But Johannes Romberg's cultured background also stood him in good stead. It enabled him to teach his children during the years when there was no school, or at least no suitable school, available. His homes, both the early one on the San Bernardo River and the later one at Black Jack Springs, Navidad, became centers of attraction for other German Texans with background and interests similar to those of the Rombergs. Of these the family of Pastor Adolf Fuchs became most closely associated with the Romberg family. Adolf Fuchs was both poet and musician. He wrote the music for much of his own poetry and set to music verses of other poets he read and liked. Two of his sons, Wilhelm and Hermann, married daughters of Johannes Romberg.

Romberg not only drew his neighbors together within a radius of ten to fifteen miles, persons of similar background, for impromptu gemütliche Abende, during which evenings the famous writers and musicians of the past and present were discussed but he also organized a modest literary club, the *Prairieblume*.

After many years of happy family life, Johannes Romberg's wife died. But even this tragic event could not break down the spirit of Johannes Romberg or cause him to withdraw within himself. He centered his affections on his children and children's children and continued to follow to the end of his life the writing of poetry.

It is interesting to note that among the descendants of the Romberg and the Fuchs families there were a number who became well known for their publications in literature and in music. Oscar Fox, nationally known musician and composer, is a grandson of Johannes Romberg and Adolph Fuchs. In the field of literature Louise Fuchs, a daughter of Johannes Romberg and a daughter-in-law of Adolf Fuchs, has written a biography. Frieda Fuchs, a granddaughter of both Johannes Romberg and Adolf Fuchs, wrote prose and poetry for German publications and, moreover, proved herself very able in collecting, translating and copying German writings. A contemporary writer, Judge John R. Fuchs, of New Braunfels, has published two books, *A Husband's Tribute to his Wife* and *Liberation from Taxation*.

From: *The American-German Review February* 1946, Pages 165-167

The Story Of The Romberg Family

by Annie Romberg

The following information was received in two letters in the fall of 1932. The first letter was from Bernhard Romberg, pastor at Teterow in Mecklenburg, Post Office Box 67337; the second was from Präpositus Franz Romberg of Dassow, Mecklenburg, Post Office Box 58750.

Two explanations should be made. A Präpositus is a higher church official in the Lutheran Church, a dean or acting superintendent. A superintendent's position is somewhat like that of a bishop in other Protestant churches. The pastor of the Lutheran Church in Germany was always a university man. He had to have a Doctor of Divinity degree before he was given a position. The pastor was employed and paid by the State. The information received in the letters mentioned above was arranged and translated as literally as possible by Annie Romberg, Denton Texas, Christmas, 1933.

Regarding the sources of the material, Pastor Franz Romberg writes:

"The records which I am sending of our ancestors I have taken mainly from the notes of my father, the Präpositus Herman Romberg of Kalkhorst, who procured a very careful collection of the annals of the family in the eighties of the last century through the help of his colleagues in Klein-Schönfeld, Alt Bukow, Waren,... Sternberg, and Boizenburg, who gladly assisted in securing the information. Besides he used Willgerott: *Die Mecklenburg-Schwerinschen Pfarren seit dem Dreiszig Jährigen Kriege* (The Pastorates of Mecklenburg-Schwerin since the Thirty Years War), a work in which one can find accurate information about every pastorate and every pastor in Mecklenburg-Schwerin.

"I would like to mention also that your great-grandfather Bernhard's sister, Sophie Dorothea Elisabeth, born 1770, married to the Gutsbesitzer Fuchs (a Gutsbesitzer is a gentleman farmer, the owner of an estate) at Malliss, had a number of children, of whom descendants are said to live in America. I have a vague recollection that my brother Johannes wrote me sometime at the end of the last century that he had met there in Texas a family by the name of Fuchs, reported to be descendants of Hans Fuchs, the second son of the above Sophie, who was forester in Hünerbusch and later pensioned forester in Boizenburg."

1. The oldest Romberg of whom we have any information, emigrated to Germany from Holland and lived in Preussisch Holland (Prussian Holland) Kreisstadt, (chief town of a district) in the Regierungsbezirk (administrative district) of Königsberg as arrendator, later in Rügenswalde, administrative district of Köslin, and in Regenswald, district of Stettin. (An arrendator is one who rents an estate belonging to the crown or an overlord.)

2. One son of this Romberg was a musician.

3. His son was Johann Romberg. According to the Klein-Schönfeld information he was organist in the district of Güllzow; according to other information he was in Schlawe, which is south of Rügenwalde.

In the church record of Schlawe is recorded: "The Kunstpfeiffer (artistic performer on a fife, maybe flute payer) Johannes Romberg, married Dorothea Ruddoffen in 1727. He had four children by her." This could have been an older brother of Pastor Johann Gottlieb

Romberg in Klein-Schönefeld, who married about 1733. The organist Johann Romberg, (See 3 above) father of Pastor Johann Gottlieb Romberg, probably died in 1749 for according to Klein-Schönefeld records his widow, Ursula Gertrude Detloff came to her son, Johann Gottlieb Romberg in Klein-Schönefeld, where she died September 2, 1757, at eighty years of age. She was therefore born in 1677 at Pritzenhagen in the parsonage in Pomerania (Hinterpommern). Her son, Johann Gottlieb, born 1708, could therefore be the younger brother of Johann Romberg, the flute player in Schlawe who as widower married a second time as early as 1727.

4. The son of the organist Johann Romberg is Johann Gottlieb Romberg, pastor in Klein-Schönefeld near Greifenhagen in Pomerania, born August 26, 1708, previously pastor in Borkenhagen at Labes, since Easter 1741 pastor at Klein-Schönefeld; he married

(1) Anna Friederike Sievert (in ???), born January 6, 1714, died October 6, 1754, age 39 years less 3 months; married

(2) Anna Dorothea Christiane Moldenhauer, daughter of the pastor Johann Friederich Moldenhauer at Mertensdorf in the Priegnitz, born November 13, 1726 at Mertensdorf. In 1735 she came as an orphan to her mother's brother, pastor Schultz at Gartz. She married the pastor Johann Gottlieb Romberg in Klein-Schönefeld in the year 1755.

By his first marriage he had 13 (14?) children, by the second, seven. At the death of his first wife he wrote in the church record: "1754. On the 6th of October on 7 Trinitatus, hor, 10-11 ante merid., my God cast me and my ten children into the deepest grief for He took from us their devoted mother and from me my dearly beloved, devout, faithful helpmate. Before the end came, her sins seemed overpowering to her, but her faith finally conquered so that she not only attained final mercy but demanded her inheritance in Heaven, as she said. Her heroic departure alone consoles me, and her love at least remains with me and mine as a blessing. Amen. Age 39 years less 3 months. The parentation (funeral rites for parent) was in charge of Binowiensis Pastor Wittig."

At the death of the second wife he wrote: "1770. The 23rd day of May hor. 10 -11 ante merid., died a faithful stepmother, Anna Dorothea Christiana, nee Moldenhauer, my beloved wife, h. e. by marriage Mrs. Pastor Romberg, of this place. She was born November 23, 1726 at Mertensdorf in the Priegnitz, came to Gartz to her mother's brother, honorary pastor (Ehrenpastor) Schultz as an orphan in 1736. In 1755 she became the mother to 10 orphans in Klein-Schönefeld. She went through her married life quietly, lovingly and industriously, through sorrow and distress calmly, more active in works than in words. She suffered through a long illness, and died in the faith of Jesus. She left 3 sons and 1 daughter. Parentation. Ebraer 11: 'All these died in the Faith.' Age 44 years."

At the death of Johann Gottlieb we read: "At Klein-Schönfeld on March 1, 1792, the Right Reverend (Hochwohlerwürden) Johann Gottlieb Romberg pastor emeritus at that place died of old age at the age of 83 years, 7 months and 5 days."

5. Johann Christlieb Romberg was born in Klein-Schönefeld August 3, 1741. Assistant pastor at St. Georgen in Parchim, 1766. Ordained on the 26th of December. Pastor in Alt Bukow in Mecklenburg-Schwerin in 1769. Präpositus 1778, August 1. Pastor emeritus May, 1806. He kept his position as Präpositus until his death, July 24, 1812 in his 71st year. Married October 24, 1769 to Dorothea Wildschenk, christened at Parchim, St.

Georqen, September 19, 1732. Dorothea Wildschenk was the daughter of a peruke [wig] maker, Daniel Gabriel Wildschenk. She died of dropsy September 27, 1785 in her 54th year.

6. His son was Bernhard Friedrich Christlieb Romberg, born at Alt Bukow May 17, 1776, christened May 19th. He became pastor in Alt Bukow as his father's successor, May 19, 1806. He died from abdominal complaint with convulsions August 25, 1822, in his 74th year. The illness and death were said to have been the result of an act of devil-banishing performed by him. In the tavern at Wartenbrugg—so goes the legend—a number of men after they had gone to confession on Saturday, as was then customary, had begun a game of cards which lasted into the next morning and beyond, and which finally caused them to miss the communion service. And so the devil had attained power over them. As one of them turned to pick up a card that had fallen under the table, all at once he with the cloven hoof sat right there grinning at him, so that the man died from terror. For some time the devil continued to play his tricks at the tavern, until Romberg, who understood thoroughly how to do a thing of that sort, banished him from the house. On the way home, however, he was followed by the devil and tormented (bedeviled) in such a manner under the Wartenbrügger bridge and later again in the Quertiner woods, that he was seized with convulsions and came home dripping with perspiration and died soon afterwards.

Bernhard Friedrich Christlieb Romberg married Conradine Sophie Friederike, nee Hast, christened at Hagenow April 5, 1779. She was the daughter of the Präpositus Johann Ulrich Christoph Hast at Hagenow in Mecklenburg-Schwerin (small city.) Married July 27, 1807. Died after a widowhood of 41 years in Hagenow

January 16, 1863, in her 84th year. One son, Johannes Christlieb Nathanael, 1808-1891.

Bernhard Romberg had an older sister Sophie Dorothea Elisabeth, born in 1770, August 25th, wife of the gentleman farmer (Gutsbesitzer) Fuchs at Malliss.

Here ends the information given in the two letters mentioned above regarding the Romberg ancestors. The rest of the story is taken from records in Texas:

Friederike Hast was anxious to study since her brothers were university students; and so she persuaded one of her brothers to tutor her. However, it was very difficult to carry out this plan; so she continued the studies by herself. It is said that she made very good progress. She married Pastor Romberg in 1807, and lived in Alt Bukow. Shortly before his death, 1822, her husband had pledged security for a friend. Later when the debt could not be paid, she kept her husband's pledge by paying with the property she had inherited from her family, even though her legal advisors explained that she could not be forced to pay. During the Napoleonic invasion, the family fled to the northern coast. Her son, Johannes, remembered this incident well. From Friederike Hast came the silverware that the family brought to Texas.

7. Johannes Christlieb Nathanael Romberg was born November 10, 1808, at Alt Bukow, where his father was pastor. He was anxious to get a university education as had been the custom in the family for generations, but his mother's fortune was gone, and besides he had poor eyesight. So it was decided by his elders that he was to become a merchant, a calling which was always very distasteful to him. For training he entered the business house of Johannes Dietrich Bauch in Schwerin. He lived in the home of his employer and pursued literary stud-

ies with the daughter, Friederike Amalie Elise Bauch. In 1833 he established himself as merchant in Boizenburg and during the same year married Friederike.

In 1847 he emigrated with his family to Texas because he hoped to provide better opportunities for his children. He settled down first near Cat Spring and later moved to Fayette County near La Grange in a community called the Latin Settlement. He was engaged there, as most people in those days, in farming and stock raising. His chief interest, however, lay in philosophy and literature. Before the Civil War he organized and promoted for a number of years in the Latin Settlement a literary society and a reading circle. Books were bought and passed from member to member. In his later years he spent most of his time writing. A collection of his poems was published in 1899. There are besides several longer narrative poems, which show his humor and his philosophy. His writings belong to the romantic period of literature. It is significant that when emigrating to the frontier land of Texas, he brought along the newest edition of Meyer's Konservationslexikon (encyclopaedia) and the classics. Died in 1891. His wife, a very congenial helpmate, was a teacher before her marriage. In Texas she taught her children and read to them at night from the classics. Died in 1883.

Children of this union were: Bernhardine, born 1834; Johannes, 1836; Bernhard , 1838 (died in infancy); Louise, 1840; Bernhard, 1841; Ida, 1843; Caroline, 1846; Friederike, 1847; and Julius, born in Texas, February 2, 1851.

www.ingramcontent.com/pod-product-compliance
Lightning Source LLC
LaVergne TN
LVHW092233110526
838202LV00092B/20